Gay and Single . . . Forever?

10 Things Every Gay Guy Looking for Love
(and Not Finding It) Needs to Know

Steven Bereznai

Marlowe & Company
New York

GAY AND SINGLE . . . FOREVER?:
10 Things Every Gay Guy Looking for Love (and Not Finding It) Needs to Know

Published by
Marlowe & Company
An Imprint of Avalon Publishing Group, Incorporated
245 West 17th Street • 11th Floor
New York, NY 10011-5300

AVALON
publishing group incorporated

Library of Congress Cataloging-in-Publication Data

Bereznai, Steven.
    Gay and single—forever? : 10 things every gay guy looking for love
(and not finding it) needs to know / Steven Bereznai.
        p. cm.
    ISBN-13: 978-1-56924-356-5 (pbk.)
    1. Gay men—Psychology. 2. Single men—Psychology. 3. Interpersonal relations.
    I. Title.

    HQ76.B447 2006
    06.81'5208664—dc22

                                                                2006018148

ISBN-10: 1-56924-356-5

9 8 7 6 5 4 3 2 1

Interior design by Maria E. Torres
Printed in the United States of America

For my dad, my mom, and my brothers, Anthony and Nicholas. When I was thirteen years old, I told you guys I'd started writing a novel. I was expecting you all to laugh. None of you did. I needed that vote of confidence, and I've kept writing ever since. Thank you with all my heart.

"The man who goes alone can start today; but he who travels with another must wait till that other is ready."

—Henry David Thoreau

Contents

Introduction

SINGLE IS THE NEW GAY

When did being alone become the modern day equivalent of being a leper? Will restaurants soon be divided up into sections? Smoking, non-smoking, single, non-single?

— Carrie Bradshaw (aka Sarah Jessica Parker),
Sex and the City

I AM A CATCH.

I have a good job. I can use power tools. I own a brand-new condo high in the sky with floor-to-ceiling windows, and my cupboards are stocked—martini glasses from Caban, gourmet cheesecake recipes from Williams-Sonoma (thank you to my friend Parker!), and I've dumped the Ikea couch in favor of a loveseat import from Montreal. The wool weave isn't brown, darling, it's *llama*.

In short, as one of my personal ads on the popular queer Web site gay.com once read: I have EQUITY. University educated, well read and traveled. I'm also funny. My improv teacher says so.

And let's be honest. I'm not sore on the eyes. I boast a waistline that's smaller than it was in high school. I get compliments on my chest and biceps. I'm versatile and my cock's bigger than a baby's arm. Well, OK, it's average. So apart from size-queens (who needs them anyway?), I've got a pretty good package.

And yet here I am, thirty-two years old, never had a boyfriend, chronically single-and-searching.

This is *not* how my life was supposed to go.

When I was nineteen I started coming out to my dorm mates during my freshmen year. As this process gained momentum, it became imperative that I tell my parents that I was gay—stat! Obviously once I started coming out, I would have a boyfriend in short order, and it would be unfair of me to expect my parents not only to open their arms to their fresh-out-of-the-closet gay son but also to enthusiastically embrace his new boyfriend at the same time.

Even as a nineteen-year-old in heat I understood that the right thing to do was to tell them I was gay, give them a bit of time to adjust, and *then* I could get into a relationship. I had to drop the pink bomb before my window of singlehood slammed shut.

Clearly there was no time to lose.

Aside from a deep blush on my mother's cheeks, and asking me three times in a row if I was "sure" (she cut herself off the third time: "You already answered that," she said more to herself than to me), all went smoothly with friends and family. In fact there were a couple of unexpected bonuses. Not only did mummy dearest take on the responsibility of coming out to my dad and older brother on my behalf, I finally no longer had to answer the dreaded question "So, do you have a girlfriend?"

Nor did they ask if there was a guy in my life, for which I was grateful. For a brief time I existed under an unspoken gay single's amnesty. Everyone was accepting of my homosexuality but just uncomfortable enough about the details to leave my dating life alone.

Until . . .

"So, are you seeing anyone?" my mother asked.

I nearly spat out my goulash.

"Too much paprika?" she inquired, her Hungarian accent indiscernible to me who'd grown up with it, but which my high school friends considered "wicked," in the good sense of the word.

On the one hand the question was a sweet gesture that indicated acceptance, but in all honesty that query made my insides shrivel when forced to reply, "No, no one special in my life. Still single. Nope, no one on the horizon. Couple of crushes. No . . . they don't know that I exist just yet, but fingers crossed."

It was in that moment that my brief relationship grace period was over. Among my friends, and within gay culture, it never existed. My straight friends would excitedly introduce me to any new gay acquaintance, simply because we were both gay and single. *Is that really the best you think I can do?* I wondered, quickly learning to thank them while demurely explaining that I do not do setups.

And there were the times when, in the midst of sex with a trick, he'd suddenly ask, "So, do you have a boyfriend?"

With my brain concentrated in the head of my erection I wondered when such questions had become casual pillow talk. I'd stammer replies intended to assuage whatever fears might be attached to my singleness, for make no mistake, this state of being perplexed them, even though it was usually another single gay man asking the question.

"But you *seem* like a great guy," he'd persist.

And for the moment of silence that inevitably followed I felt as if they were waiting for me to rip off my mask and reveal my horrible defect.

Now, as I look toward the next ten years and beyond, I begin to wonder, what if this is it? What if Singlesville is my final destination? Is there room for me in a post-Stonewall era, where the push to partner with a man has replaced the pressure to marry a woman? Where being gay is fine but the answer "No, I'm not dating anyone" receives looks of pity, and in my mom's eyes, fear that I will grow old and lonely, dying of AIDS from a presumed life of unsafe promiscuity? Again, not because I'm gay, but because I'm *single* and gay, and the old bird knows I must be getting my rocks off somehow.

Or maybe I'm projecting.

Maybe that's what I fear for myself.

And what if there *is* something wrong with me? Maybe I'm too materialistic. Or conceited. On the other hand, that could just be my cover for low self-esteem. Or maybe my personality's deficient. What if my smarts, looks, and wit simply aren't up to snuff? In retrospect, my improv teacher didn't say I was funny so much as she said I was good at following instructions.

Maybe I *am* damaged.

What then?

The more I grapple with these very real questions the more I find there are actual answers. Some are amorphous, others refreshingly simple, at least until they are applied to an uncooperative world that feels to me like an ever shifting board game, Monopoly meets Life meets you sank my Battleship!, except all the players each seem to be following a different set of rules, moment to moment.

I'm referring of course to the former fuck buddy who fell through just when I was finally coming around to once more accepting his advances, to the best friend who had the nerve to get into a relationship and put his boyfriend's emotional needs ahead of mine, and let's not forget the biggest bitch of them all: HIV, raising the stakes and challenges in a sexual subculture where many recognize that to slide into a guy, or to be slid into, skin to skin, flesh to flesh, whatever the consequences, *feels* better than being sheathed, at least in the moment.

It can be ecstasy. Literally, figuratively, or in a pill. At other times, like a bad case of nonspecific urethritis, it *burns*.

And regardless of what Nietzsche might say, sometimes whatever doesn't kill you doesn't make you stronger. It just makes you limp.

And yet, even as I hobble across this minefield of gay love, putting my battered body, heart, and soul at ever increasing risks, my stride lengthens, my confidence rises, my chakras grow strong.

Pourquoi?

Because to stay put, or worse, move backward, is, like quivering in the closet, far worse than facing whatever lies ahead.

And so I remove my emotional armor piece by piece, in therapy, in bars, in weekend naked workshops, with companions in the life, in improv class, with sex workers, on party drugs, in the arms of one-night stands and three-week fucks. How else do I get to the tender spots I once hoped a boyfriend would reach for me? And as this book has progressed I have felt a growing sense of peace. Thank you yoga and *Spirituality for Dummies*. It's a quiet yet powerful feeling emanating from a powerful realization.

Single is the new gay.

This is not an all-encompassing truth, but there are striking parallels between the stigma of homos and that of singlehood, from their origins to identity politics to the role of nature versus nurture, not to mention the increasing pressure to pair with a man as the stigma of not marrying a woman decreases.

Clearly this thesis requires and assumes a certain level of acceptance of homosexuality as legitimate and moral and equal to heterosexuality. Obviously, this is not a universal understanding. As of print time there is not, and never has been, an openly gay athlete competing in the NHL or NFL. Olympic ice skaters are afraid to publicly come out. More severe, according to the International Gay and Lesbian Human Rights Commission, eighty-four countries have laws criminalizing sexual acts between adults in private. During Jerusalem's 2005 Pride march, a stabber attacked three people. Amnesty International cites instances in Jamaica of gays and lesbians being murdered, raped, or chased from their homes or communities. In 2001 a gay man was beaten to death while cruising in Vancouver's Stanley Park. In Wyoming, in 1998, twenty-one-year-old Matthew Sheppard was beaten with a pistol, tortured, and tied to a fence for eighteen hours. He died five days later.

It almost seems in poor taste, and borderline whiney, to even be discussing gay singlehood as an issue beyond dinner-party kvetching. But then the same would have to be said about gay marriage. Battling for wedding bands, legal partner recognition, and a potential tax break can seem trivial when in some milieus fags and dykes fear and fight for their lives. And yet at the end of the day, the struggle is the same: for equality. The enemy is the same: fear and hate.

Different battles, same war.

Unfortunately, it is within those public and private arenas where homosexuality *has* gained status, be they professional or personal, group or individual, a micro- or macrocosm, that single is the brand many of us now carry, the abnormal status we struggle with. It is in this sense that I find single is the new gay. Of course for straights it has long been thus, and the long tradition of associating singlehood and homosexuality (i.e., if you're single, you're gay) was used to establish a double pariah status within straight society.

The tables have now turned.

In the shadow of gay marriage, and our fight for equality, many of our more amorphous intimacies no longer receive their due, from tricks to fuck buddies to mentors and friends. The result? More and more single gay men are buffeted by a variety of internal and external forces to buddy up, oftentimes with consequences for the gay single not unlike those of the closet: a sense of shame, failure, and a quiet (or not so quiet) desperation.

And yet for all that, up to 60 percent of gay men remain single. Some are happily so, but many of us struggle to reconcile ourselves with this "freakish" state.

In terms of defining what I mean by single, I turn to the groundbreaking research of Andrew Hostetler, who has done

the first focused study on how some gay singles have negotiated a sense of psychological well-being in a world that pressures them to couple. With few exceptions his research
subjects interpreted single as being "without a long-term (primary) relationship," and those who described themselves as
single were generally saying that they were "without a partner
or significant other."

Works for me.

According to Hostetler's 2001 study, "Single Gay Men: Cultural Models of Adult Development, Psychological Well-
Being, and the Meaning of Being 'Single by Choice,'" the
happiest among these gay men are those who have chosen to
be so. Going through Hostetler's dissertation, prepared for the
University of Chicago, I think what the Kinsey Report did for
sexuality in the '50s, maybe Hostetler can do for single gay
men in the new millennium. The beauty of the Kinsey Report,
and part of why it is still widely referred to today, is that it
didn't look for neuroses or pathology in people's sexuality.
Instead of looking at what people were doing "wrong" sexually, it simply asked "What are people doing?" By taking this
angle, it expanded the range of acceptable sexual practices by
making private acts publicly known.

So while Hostetler explores his thesis that those gay men who
are "single by choice" will be happier than those who are single
against their wishes, a key part of his research is simply looking at
how these men are living their lives without imposing societal
assumptions on them that they *should* be in a couple.

The comparison to Kinsey underlines the philosophy that I, with all my own predispositions, have tried to use in thinking about, researching, and writing this book. Having said that, I do have to be honest about one major bias. Just as books about gay relationships (getting one or staying in one) focus on couplehood and only have a few lines about singles who are not looking for a relationship, I reversed the ratios for this work, specifically focusing on men who have reached a level of peace and comfort with their singlehood, rather than those desperately seeking couplehood.

I have interviewed dozens of men, most of them over a six-month period, focusing on the alternatives gay men have invested in for building companionship, sex, and intimacy outside the framework of a traditional relationship. This is not to say that these gay singles don't face challenges or moments of loneliness. This is part of being human. But they have much to offer in terms of finding and enjoying love, sex, and intimacy in a world that believes in Mr. Right, but which often fails to provide him.

With these individuals' help, I have cobbled together a map to help guide me through the danger zones of the gay lovescape. With their counsel, and through the twists and turns of history, biology, psychology, and sociology, I've isolated ten things that gay men, single or otherwise, *must* know about love and relationships to more fully open themselves to a fruitful and satisfying life.

From "Gay Is Good—Being Gay and Single Used to Be,

Too," to "Boyfriends and Husbands Don't Protect against AIDS," I find myself rereading these "rules" in my darker moments as signposts toward the light. And yes, there are still moments of struggle, and the odd crush that gets me practicing wedding vows in my head. That should come as no surprise.

After all, in any quest of *Lord of the Rings* proportions (hello Frodo and his "friend" Sam), one inevitably finds oneself at the top of a volcano, turning into a total bitch over a fucking ring that makes one invisible.

And it really does feel like the fate of one's inner Middle Earth is at stake.

In a way it is, for the question of being single forever is not an idle one. It can strike at the heart of one's assumptions of one's life course, where one ought to be by a certain age, and fundamentally it forces one to ponder how one intends to spend one's life without the underlying assumption of coupledom.

But enough of the shire.

Just as *The Lord of the Rings* does not begin at the beginning, neither does this tale.

It's time for the back story.

1.

Gay is Good— Being Gay and Single Used to Be, Too

If we can't deal with the past, we'll never understand the present. If you don't understand the present, then you drown in it.

— James Baldwin,
The Advocate, May 27, 1986

I T'S WHAT I WANT, for now."

After a decade of living in Canada's largest city as a single gay man, that's the answer I give when people ask me why I'm single. I say this because I have to say something that will throw them off the scent of my quiet desperation to find a guy. They want reassurance almost as much as I do that I am not wallowing in loneliness. They know as well as I do that being single is a bad thing and they need some sign that this state is temporary.

So I tell them what they want to hear.

But it is the little lie that leads to the bigger ones.

The truth is, after completing my degree at twenty-two I moved from a smallish town to the big city "to fall in love."

Like many a young gay lad entering a bustling metropolis, I bought my first gay uniform. A tight black T-shirt and designer jeans replaced my lesbian plaid lumberjack look, and my puffy hair got clipped and spiked. In the boy bars I taught myself to cruise successfully and date unsuccessfully. My carbs went up, then down, now up again in an attempt to fill out my shoulders and ass. Online, I learned not to refer to myself as tall and lanky. Swimmer's build, I insist.

And it was in this ecosystem that I finally snapped, specifically at an alterna-queer-dance night at Toronto's Buddies in Bad Times Theatre. I was in my midtwenties. "Independent Women" by Destiny's Child was at the top of the Billboard charts, and smoking was still allowed in the city's clubs.

This white guy had been giving me the lazy eye for about half-an-hour. He wore a body-hugging long-sleeved green shirt. Cropped hair. Sensuous lips. I casually let my Ping Pong gaze bounce back and forth a couple of times, lingering just so.

He introduced himself to me at the bar.

After a few minutes of idle chat he proclaimed, "So you

must be in a relationship . . . or there's something wrong with you."

And there it was. The old catch-22. You can't get the job without experience, and without experience you can't get the job. Not only that, it mirrored a growing lesson. Gay was good, but gay and *single* was bad. Anger fought with desperation. The bitchy queen who leveled high school homophobes with her acidic tongue rose to the fore, planning to decimate this ingrate with her sarcasm.

"There *is* something wrong with me," I wanted to say. "I have a small cock. And I'm *really* bad in bed." Then again, I'd had enough mediocre sex with other people's boyfriends to know that being a good lover was *not* a prerequisite to landing a relationship. Or staying in one.

And so my anger deflated. Like a closeted high school fairy amid a group of menacing jocks (whose approval I so desperately wanted), I was not about to stand up for singlehood. So what would I say?

"It's what I want" inevitably rang hollow. Nor was saying this getting me off the loser team. So like a desperate job hunter, I lied on my résumé. I knew I'd make for a good boyfriend. I knew I could be that person. I just needed one attractive-enough guy to give me a chance, and then I'd have a real relationship to put on my CV.

"I had a boyfriend," I lied. "But we broke up."

And that's the moment I opened the door and stepped into the singles' closet.

"Really?" he asked. His feet didn't move, but with a slight arching of the back his torso cautiously began to retreat. "How long ago was that?"

I could see his doubt and fear. He believed I was on the rebound. The Geiger counter in his mind was going ballistic, reading me as toxic waste almost as deadly as the chronically single man that I still am.

One lie led to two.

"It ended six months ago. He moved to Vancouver. It was an amicable split. We were only together half-a-year anyway."

The delivery was nonchalant. "No baggage here" was the subtext I tried to convey. There was relief in the eyes of Mr. Buddies in Bad Times and his posture relaxed, inclining slightly toward me. It would seem I was finally learning the language of gay courtship.

But I was far from fluent.

Oh, sure, his tongue wound up in my mouth. Mine in his. We even went on a date a week later. At evening's end he stood at my door, bidding me good night, and I made what I thought was an offhand comment, one that I could've totally sworn was in context of the discussion we'd been having.

"If a guy's not looking for a boyfriend, then he's wasting my time," I said.

There was no second date after that.

His promise to call soon expired. Too much pressure, he explained when we ran into each other on the street months later.

When I meet a guy I'm attracted to, I don't mention wanting a boyfriend anymore. The old saying goes that you find a boyfriend when you're not looking. But that's not true. I've stopped looking lots of times, and nada. But I've never stopped *wanting*. To get what I wanted it seemed I had to stop wanting what I wanted. The closest I could manage was to shut up about it in the hopes of not scaring guys away.

But when I became interested my enthusiasm always seemed to shine through.

With each rejection the light grew a little dimmer, but it never extinguished. And I sometimes wonder why that little flicker still remains.

I think it has to do with the belief that if I am a good person I will one day find someone suitable who sees that, and who will acknowledge and love those unique elements of my inner being. And I do believe that I'm a good person. I know this. I'm not a perfect person. But I am a good person. I am "boyfriend material," that highest of high praise.

And so that flicker of light remains, even *without* a boyfriend to validate it. And if this is to be my state forever? Instead of waiting around to have a boyfriend to prove that I'm "worthy," to myself and to the rest of the world, I am learning to no longer use "boyfriend material" as my litmus-test lingo. I phrase it differently now.

I am a good man.

I am a good gay man.

I am a good single gay man.

Singlehood Does *Not* Equal Failure

In this world a lot of emphasis is put on being "good enough" that someone might actually want to date you. In fact there's so much pressure there are times when it's hard to remember that singlehood is not failurehood.

It's been almost a decade since I graduated with an environmental science degree, founding an environmental residence at my alma mater along the way, not to mention guiding a number of fledgling queers out of the closet and successfully pursuing a journalism career beyond those academic halls. Still, I sometimes wonder if I've somehow failed at life on a very primal level.

The equation used to look like this:

Gay = single = alone = lonely = dysfunctional.

Now that GAY has been removed from the computation in at least some circles, the formula is:

Single = alone = lonely = dysfunctional.

"Gay is good" is no longer good enough to claim a positive identity beyond the sexual stigmatization of one's youth. Now equality is part of a relationship package.

And here I sit, in the metaphoric cold, in my metaphoric winter jacket, holding out my metaphoric tin cup, worthy of looks of pity and perhaps a metaphoric hot meal at the local metaphoric homeless shelter.

That is what often rings behind the question "Why are you single?"

It asks not only "What's wrong with you?" but "Why have you flopped?"

Even without someone prompting such doubts, they buzz around me when I experience a significant lull from the distraction of overworking or overplaying.

Where did I go wrong?

How do I get it right?

Fortunately there is another voice, too quiet at times, but growing louder. It tells the chatter to *shut the fuck up.*

It also reminds me that for one decade, there was a different formula.

Gay + Single = Good

And when I remember that, I know that I am not delusional in believing I can be gay and single, maybe forever, and a worthy self-realized human being at the same time.

Enter the 1970s.

Singlehood Comes Out of the Closet

Gay rights raged into the '70s as a group of drag queens, dykes, and bar boys fought back with beer bottles, bricks, and campy catcalls during a police raid on the New York bar known as the Stonewall Inn. It happened on the night of June 27, 1969. Gay icon Judy Garland had been buried earlier that day. Many gay bars in Greenwich Village were draped in black. The queens, many of them black or Latino, were in no mood to put up with police bullshit.

The newsletter of the Mattachine Society of New York, one of the earliest homophile organizations in the United States, described the rebellion as "the hairpin drop heard round the world."

Queers had shrugged off the accommodating tactics that had come to dominate the homophile movements of the '50s and '60s, which attempted to strike a delicate balance between staying under the radar and pinning their hopes on eventual respectability. Out of fear of being crushed by a virulently antigay government, many gay rights activists shied away from outright rebellion and gambled that conformity would lead to toleration. But by the end of the '60s queers no longer politely stood on the sidelines as militancy swept through the women's, civil rights, and antiwar movements.

Connections were also being made between various forms of oppression. Just as Frank Kameny's 1960's battle cry "Gay is Good" was inspired by "Black is Beautiful," gays succeeded in winning greater liberties for queers by piggybacking on the gains of the black movement and pushing for amendments to existing civil rights laws originally designed to protect African-Americans. The Supreme Commander of the Black Panther Party published a letter stating, "the women's liberation front and gay liberation front are our friends." If there had been a singles liberation front, it could have piped up and asked to be included as well.

In a way, gays were in fact that voice.

Down with Marriage

In the '50s the word *bachelor* remained a euphemism for homosexual, linking together two socially deviant lifestyles, making them one and the same. The gay movement of the

'70s did something quite remarkable in not trying to separate the two, for it recognized that the stigma of homos and singles were twin oppressions from a single source—heterosexual couplehood—and so took aim at many of the assumptions of marriage and other forms of traditional pair bonds.

In his early-'70s *Gay Manifesto,* Carl Wittman summed up this philosophy:

"Traditional marriage is a rotten, oppressive institution . . . marriage is a contract which smothers both people, denies needs, and places impossible demands on both people." His list of things to "get away from" includes: "exclusiveness, propertied attitudes toward each other, a mutual pact [presumably between spouses] against the rest of the world."

Gary Kinsman, now a sociologist at Ontario's Laurentian University and the author of *The Regulation of Desire: Homo and Hetero Sexualities,* was a significant player in Toronto's gay liberation movement in the '70s and has witnessed firsthand how things have changed.

"If someone had told me in the 1970s that a major part of gay liberation in the '90s would be gay marriage, I would have laughed," Kinsman says.

Back in the day, he tells me, the public slogans included "smash monogamy." "At that point in time," he says, "there was much more validation and affirmation of being single."

In *The Rise of a Gay and Lesbian Movement,* Barry D. Adam describes a revolutionary struggle that challenged any attempts to limit sexuality to monogamous heterosexual families, a movement which actively raged "against a repressive order of marriage, oedipal families, and compulsive heterosexuality."

So the next time someone at a bar asks me why I am single, I'll just reply that I'm raging against the oedipal family complex and compulsive hetero paradigms. The object of my desire will no doubt cautiously step back, lean over to his friend, and whisper about me, referring to me as a bitter lesbian who's been brainwashed by academia and who's now tragically become trapped in a gay man's body. They'll politely excuse themselves, shaking their heads in pity as they wander into the throng and avoid making eye contact with me for the rest of the night. I, in turn, will down my green apple sour martini and know exactly why I'm single.

In other words, slogans can only go so far, but as someone born in 1973, I do marvel at the way queers stepped up to the plate and took their shot at changing America instead of fitting into it. That needs not only to be recognized but used as something of an inspiration. The love that dared not speak its name became the love that would not shut up. Gay was good. So was being single. This is a revolutionary concept, one that for straights was countercultural but for gays was at the heart of their budding communities.

Beyond Chants and Mantras

So how did this play out in the streets and between the sheets?

A closer look at the '70s reveals much richer and complicated negotiations of sex and love within newfound liberty than can be summarized in a few mantras. This era should not be revisited with rose-colored glasses or wistful thinking of the good old days as we sit in our rockers on a porch in an old-age home in Florida.

It may even have been taken too far, at least within the court of public opinion. Enter Larry Kramer's best-selling novel *Faggots*. Described by *Publishers Weekly* as "the quintessential homosexual 'how-to' manual," it pits main character Fred Lemmish against the '70s gay-boy party mecca of New York and Fire Island. He's finally gotten himself into a state of fatless great shape. He's become "a number," and now his quest can proceed: to find true love in three days before he turns forty.

We first meet him in Chelsea, at the Everhard Baths, on the cusp of a piss scene.

Near novel's end he watches the love of his life getting publicly fist fucked while riding a log held aloft by two ropes. At last Lemmish concludes, "I know what I want and I ain't gettin' it. I say I'm settling for too fucking little. I say the whole set-up I've set up is out to sabotage me. I say I'm not going to find love here. And even if I could, how could it survive and grow?"

If Kramer was struggling with the tension between a relationship and sexual excess, in *Faggots* he clearly comes out in favor of a relationship, and paid a social price when the novel was first released. Friends stopped talking with him and would cross the street if they saw him coming. He was even asked not to come back to gay summer retreat the Pines. And he was not the only one to be highly criticized for an artistic vision that many interpreted as perpetuating straight ideals of couplehood. When the Tony Award–winning play *Torch Song Trilogy* first came out, playwright and actor Harvey Fierstein says in the commentary for the movie version that he was attacked by many people in the gay community for wanting to write about monogamy, as well as gay men adopting kids.

"We don't want to be like heterosexuals. We don't want to be in a marriage," he was told.

But as he also points out, look where we are now.

"It's sort of interesting that the arguments that *Torch Song* made, the gay community would be on the opposite side now. . . . Straights always criticized us for being overly sexually active and all that, now we're being criticized for wanting to get married. It was the opposite with the gay community."

So how useful is any of this today?

Times have changed and the ratio of singles positivism to singles negativism has flipped, and the battle cries and mores that developed in the disco Crisco era may be somewhat dated. But they are not entirely obsolete, and for gay and single to be good again, they need something of a resurgence to counterbalance the growing weight of gay relationship-centrism. Case in point: when I first left the closet in 1992, in my mind, Coming Out *equaled* boyfriend.

I had visions of walking hand in hand with my guy to the farmers' market to pick up a loaf of blueberry bread from a local Mennonite baker, and then we'd go home to cuddle and read on a worn but comfortable sofa that screamed student chic. I was disappointed by my reality. For much of high school I sat on the sidelines and watched my straight peers date up a storm. That I could accept. After all, I was still in the closet, so who would I date? And yet even after joining gay society, I was *still* on the fringe, witnessing guys come out *after* me and getting into relationships *before* me.

Stop jumping the bloody queue! I wanted to shout.

For the current generation, I believe coming out and coupling have become even more closely enmeshed.

"We're Generation-M," my twenty-one-year-old friend Michael Pihach quips without a trace of irony, referring to the marriage obsession of numbers of gay guys in his age group, who have been bombarded with images of gay matrimony on TV in their formative teen years. As the "Together" columnist of Toronto's gay scene magazine *fab* he interviews couple after couple, issue after issue. And as a self-avowed twink, he knows of what he speaks.

But as a thirty-two-year-old, I'm now looking to the '70s to help me start disentangling the overly enmeshed states of gayhood and gay couplehood and to stop thinking of them as one and the same. I want to know my place not as a gay man but as a *single* gay man, and how that can be a good thing.

What Gay Singlehood Was *Really* Like

The '70s have become known as the golden age of promiscuity. The literati of the day, such as Andrew Holleran, Larry

Kramer, and Edmund White, were certainly covering this scene. From bar culture to anonymous hookups, they told tales rife with fist fucking, hard bodies, quick encounters, endless pining, hard drugs, and the shame of a small cock. The magazine where many writers of their ilk got their first chance to really delve into the lives of gay men was *Christopher Street*. At a time when the magazine was being processed on an IBM that only had enough memory to store just over five pages of text at once, *CS* was the most prominent gay publication of the era, alongside the *Advocate*. Someone allegedly described *CS* to Gore Vidal as "a gay *New Yorker*." Vidal replied, "then what's the *New Yorker*?"

As a sign of the times, the cover of the May 1978 issue of *Christopher Street* took a look at surging bar life, depicting a young man with a mustache leaning against a plain backdrop, smoking a cigarette, and holding a bottle of beer. He wears a plaid shirt and has a Ken-doll haircut. Next to him the words "Have you been standing in the same place in the same bar, drinking the same drink for the last two years? Do others at the bar think you have a clone? Maybe you have EVERY NIGHT FEVER."

The other big story: "Hepatitis Vaccine: A Medical Breakthrough for Gay Men."

I turn to *CS* to get a better sense of what gay life, and hence gay singlehood, was *really* like beyond activist chants and denouncements of easy targets like Larry Kramer and Harvey Fierstein.

My hope is to separate the myths of the time from the day-to-day reality of gay love and get a clearer glimpse of how a microsociety that valued singlehood functioned on the level of the individual.

For some within the gay community bar life *became* life. For others, there remained a newness to much of the more outré activity. In *CS* (March 1978), a skeptical Seymour Kleinberg decided to check out New York's infamous Anvil Bar to see if the tales of debauchery were true. He says the bar had put a stop to spontaneous fist-fucking demonstrations because it attracted too many "tourists" from the uptown discos, but otherwise the fuck room, the flickering hard-core porn, and the go-go boys, naked except for cock rings and work boots, all lived up to reputation.

Beyond bars, *CS* tapped into the day-to-day travails of gay courtship and domesticity, getting to the heart of the relationship issue with banal questions like "Who does the cooking?"

I track down about a decade's worth of the magazine at the University of Toronto's Robarts Library. The library's basement washroom was once rumored to be a great cruising area. I find myself seated amid the book stacks on the eleventh floor, wondering if I'll run into the cute varsity rower I've chatted with a couple of times on gay.com and MSN.

No such luck. I return to my magazines of gay times long gone.

In 1977 the editors of *CS* ran a particularly amusing series called "My First Love," by Richard Friedel, whose novel *The Movie Lover,* published in 1981, was, along with *Dancer from the Dance* and *Faggots,* one of the first to address gay themes with total candor. He tells the nightmare of dating a fellow named Winston who would disappear for hours when he'd pop out to buy cigarettes.

"I'd ask him if there was some reason he was putting on a cock ring to do this. Winston did not like answering questions of this nature."

On this very day-to-day level, outside the spotlight of activist rhetoric, the reality of gay sex and relationships played out, from the slutty to the devoted. This is important to keep in mind before getting carried away by any '70s singles' credo.

"I never felt people were judging me for being monogamous," longtime *CS* editor Tom Steele tells me from his home in Manhattan's East Village. At fifty-three, he's now a cookbook author and culinary journalist, but he remembers well his own seven-year relationship that began when he was eighteen. Despite the promiscuity of the time, he says it was, ironically, the only one of his many past relationships in which he was monogamous (at least for five of the seven years they were together). There was some criticism, but much more muted and much less political than what more public targets endured. "Sometimes people talked to me about aping heterosexuals," says Steele. "But it turns out it's because I was cute and they wanted to fuck me."

With that simple statement he cuts through dogmatic slogans and highbrow literature. Men are men, and that's what much of this boils down to. So let's really boil it down, sulfuric-acid style.

Many of the men I spoke with who were part of the gay community in those days were very insistent on telling me that gay men *did* look for relationships in the '70s. I ask Tom Steele what I asked each of those guys: "But did anyone ever ask *why are you single?*"

Their answer was consistent across the board.

Never.

Now that's liberation.

Why?

If I'd come of age in the '70s, I would not have had to justify my existence over and over again to gays and straights alike just because I did not have a boyfriend. I would not have had to lie and say "it's a phase" to put people at ease. And while my merit might still be judged by who I had on my arm in the moment, at least I would not be judged for *not* having someone there at all. I would not be a failure. I could be good, I could be "boyfriend material," *and* I could be single.

Forever.

Commitment vs. Sexual Freedom

Having said all that, I do not want to oversimplify. With people being people, there was still plenty of psycho-emotional turmoil brewing within the psyches of 1970s single gay men, even if the social pressure to pair up was not present within the gay community.

Within 1970's urban gay sexual culture a central tension emerged that I still see in the gay culture of today, and have felt myself, and that at times definitely leaves me wanting to get into a long-term relationship. Edmund White summed up the dilemma of love and sex when he wrote about 1970s gay Manhattan in his 1997 novel *The Farewell Symphony*.

"I'd had sex with my first thousand men but that was a statistic that might sound like an achievement more to someone else than to me," White writes. "Sex is an appetite that must be fed every day; even a thousand past banquets cannot nourish the body tomorrow. I was longing for the thousand and first knight whom at last I would marry and with whom I'd live ever after in the strictest of fidelity. If marriage was my conscious but still deferred goal, I was less ready to admit I was always on the lookout for adventure."

And this was not the inner monologue of one gay writer alone. This inner tug-of-war was reflected in the population at large in the findings of James Spada's revealing 1979 survey of gay sexuality, *The Spada Report*. Spada's goal was to articulate "what it means to be a gay person today." He was more interested in qualitative than quantitative data, so his percentages should be viewed with caution. Still, *The Spada Report* details the results of a survey of just over one thousand gay men throughout the United States, with questions focusing on their hopes and feelings when it comes to relationships, sex, and the desire for intimacy.

According to Spada's findings, 52 percent of the men surveyed liked one-night stands, and "many men" enjoyed the variety of a large number of sexual partners, but "most of the men in this survey said that they view every individual as a possible relationship, whether as a lover or as a friend." And according to the 1977 breakthrough study *The Gay Report*, the first comprehensive survey to be taken in the gay community, even at a time where activists raged against oedipal families, 46 percent of gay men were in favor of marriage.

The Pressure to Pair

What I take from these studies is that gay singlehood is not a manifesto that can be spray-painted on a placard during a march on Washington. If the central tension between singlehood and being in a relationship was prevalent among half of gay men in the sex-positive '70s, it is unrealistic to think this yearning is going to disappear within the psyches of many individuals in the relationship-oriented millennium. Certainly in the conversations I had with happily single gay men, for most of them the door was still open to a relationship if "the right guy came along." Even in arguing over the title of this book, *Gay and Single . . . Forever?* won over *Gay and Single. Forever.* There is almost always a question mark, even with some of the most devoutly single gay men.

But is this question mark a reflection of *true* desire for a relationship or the lingering uncertainty from the relationship propaganda that surrounds us? Even in the 1970s there was external pressure bearing on gay men to want a relationship. One man who participated in the *The Gay Report* wrote, "Society has told me to want [a long-term relationship] and I can't escape the media pressure [presumably straight] to have one. Couples make me feel worse about being single than I would otherwise."

So even when gay and single was good, at least some people were pressured into feeling bad. More than thirty years later this is a booming industry, with books on getting into a gay relationship selling like gangbusters. Clearly gay men think more than ever that they want to get into a relationship, and feel even worse about not being in one. But interestingly, perhaps not quite bad enough. As the '70s so graphically demonstrates, the pendulum never swings just one way. Perhaps what's changed more than anything is gay men's public desire for a relationship. On the inside, during more candid conversations, many gay men, single and otherwise, remain torn between relationships and singlehood, just as they were in an earlier era.

Queer writer, activist, and professor Michael Bronski goes so far as to theorize that all the sex and S/M in the '70s (gay porn back then was boring compared to gay men's real lives) may simply have been one of the more extreme methods of negotiating the push and pull between newfound liberty and a desire for some sort of security and safety within this emotionally charged landscape of sexual exploration. In other words, literal restraints instead of symbolic ones.

I spoke with Bronski from his home in Boston as he prepared for a new semester at Dartmouth, where he's been a visiting professor for the past five years, in women's and gender studies. He's also written several books, including *The Pleasure Principle* and *Culture Clash: The Making of a Gay Sensibility.*

As a former habitué of S/M clubs like the Black and Blue and the Handball Express (in the foreword to Patrick Moore's book *Beyond Shame*, Bronski points out the names were descriptive, not metaphoric, though an evening at the B&B often ended with "Over the Rainbow" blaring from the speakers as the lights came up) he speculates that part of the draw for gay men was the immediacy of S/M acts and scenes in the sharing and giving up of power.

"The idea that you could actually have power as a gay men or as a lesbian was a new thing," Bronski tells me. "I've speculated in print that the attraction to leather and S/M, playing with those power dynamics, became attractive in the '70s because people had power for the first time and didn't know what to do with it in a safe way. And with S/M you get to have sex, too, and once you add sex to anything you can sell Tupperware with it. Clearly people did it because they were turned on, but there's usually other levels of psychic engagement."

In today's budding generation, among his students, he observes the reverse struggle as they negotiate their physical desires in a relationship-centric culture.

"Young people feel this mandate to get married, but they don't know what to do with that because they want to sleep with everyone on campus."

Again this highlights the difference between what gays might be saying, what they are actually doing, and what they might really want. In the previously cited studies on the lives of gay men in the '70s, participants spoke favorably about relationships even while tricking to the point where some felt "fagged out." Today, private and public opinions may simply have been flipped. Amid current relationship mania, and despite the public cries of "I want a boyfriend" and "Why are you single?" several studies indicate that 40 to 60 percent of contemporary gay men are still single, a much higher percentage than for straights or lesbians. I'm taking some liberties in what I make of those numbers, but maybe even in a relationship-centric culture, even while gay men might be looking for a relationship, even while they are saying they are open to a relationship, maybe even while truly believing they want a relationship, even while a relationship may in fact be right for *some* people, on some level maybe a lot of gay men just don't feel that this state is right for them.

Deep down, perhaps the real reason they are single is that they are living a higher truth, the same one that was once the dominant public voice:

Gay and single is good.

2. There Is a Conspiracy

Until they become conscious they will never rebel,
and until after they have rebelled they cannot become
conscious.

—George Orwell, *1984*

S O GAY AND SINGLE is good.

Who knows, maybe it's good enough to be single forever.

OK. But . . . how do I break it to my mom?

More importantly, how do I get her to stop asking me if I'm seeing anybody? I once tried assuring her that if I started dating someone seriously, I'd let her know. Otherwise, assume I'm not. It's a really safe bet.

"So are you seeing anyone?" she asked a week later.

It took me a while to figure out why she couldn't let this question go. Part of it is that homo-accepting moms generally want their boys in relationships, just as homo-accepting people in general want their homos in relationships, because that's what heteros want for each other. Am I paranoid in calling this a conspiracy? Most of my straight female friends wouldn't say so. This pressure to pair from those around us is part and parcel of how the conspiracy works. But I also realized that there was more to my mom's question than this. Between my dad, myself and my two brothers, she's surrounded by men who often won't tell her anything.

So I told her about the crush I had on a guy known to my friends only as "Pharmacist."

"We're in love," I assured her.

"Really?"

"Well . . . I think he knows my first name."

So we joke around about the guys who are *not* in my life. Sadly, this meant several months later I had to break it to her that things between me and Pharmacist were not working out. He now knew my name, and didn't seem particularly interested in knowing a whole lot more. Fortunately, Mom wasn't just looking for talk of happy times. Mostly she just wanted to know what was going on in my life, period.

Instead of waiting to have a guy whom I'm going to bring

home for Christmas before letting her know about him, I now fill her in on the bumps along the highway of my life. She likes hearing these tales. Makes her feel involved. And *then* she asks if I have a boyfriend.

The conspiracy is strong in her, and little wonder. We grow up with the conspiracy from the moment anyone suggests that we will get first into a heterosexual relationship, followed by a shift to a gay relationship for those of us who come out into an accepting environment. I'm now even being saddled with the possibility of a kid. "There's always adoption," I'm assured. Ironically, the conspiracy that's pressuring gays to pair (and to become parents in some instances) is tightly enmeshed in our history and culture, in a *very* antigay way. Gay is good has been absorbed into and accommodated by the relationship conspiracy, but single is good continuously gets crushed by its ever grinding wheel.

The Origin of the Conspiracy

There are those who would argue that I'm full of nonsense and that if there is any kind of relationship conspiracy, it is aimed against homosexual couples, not homosexual singles. There is, after all, a long narrative of telling gays they can't maintain long-term relationships, and the ones that do form, don't count. At least not the way straight ones do.

But this is not an argument against the anti-singles conspiracy. It is in fact where the conspiracy begins.

"The Roman emperor Augustus made a point of publicly

berating his unmarried knights, calling them—among other things—'debased pederasts who slake their filthy lusts on their slave boys,'" writes John Goodwin in *The Mating Trade.* Goodwin's book, published in 1977, was aimed primarily at a straight audience, touting itself as "the first comprehensive, behind-the-scenes, personal view of organized dating in today's America."

This sums up the conspiracy as it used to be, using the stigma of homosexuality to shame men of marrying age into a hetero-union. Campaigns using queer baiting became much more sophisticated and alarmist in later times.

Fast forward to the 1940s and 1950s.

The Push for Domesticity

There's been much documentation on the effects of the Second World War on gay American culture. The mobilization of millions of young people, including gays, took them from their small towns, introduced them to city life away from home as well as more sexually liberated attitudes in Europe, and put them in exclusively homosocial environments for the first time. For the homo-oriented among them, suddenly they had access and exposure to others like themselves. When the war ended many of them chose to remain in or relocate to major urban centers and live more openly, without a "double life."

But ultimately gays became ammunition in the conspiracy's anti-singles firing squad.

Following the social and gender upheaval of the war, and the Depression that preceded it (where both marriage and birth rates dropped as young men and women struggled financially and thus postponed forming new families), there was a strong postwar move to restore a form of hetero-domestic tranquility.

Financial incentives encouraged young men to start families and take on the role of husband and father. Such policies were innocuous enough, but as pioneering gay activist John D'Emilio points out in his series of historical essays *Making Trouble,* "other measures fell on the side of coercion, psychological or otherwise.

"Women faced a barrage of propaganda informing them that their jobs really belonged to men and extolling the virtues of marriage and child rearing. In the media, pictures of sparkling, well-equipped kitchens occupied by young mothers with babies dangling from their arms replaced images of women in hardhats surrounded by heavy machinery. . . . Where these methods failed, employers could simply fire women. . . . From 1944 to 1946, the number of women workers fell by four million."

The conspiracy was hard work.

Subversives of any kind were the enemy, including communists and other "perverts." Even sporting "unorthodox styles of dress" made one suspect, sounding a lavender alarm.

A 1941 *Newsweek* article titled "Queer People" named homosexuals as "sex murderers," "echoing a consistent media theme identifying homosexuals as destroyers of society," writes Barry D. Adam in *The Rise of a Gay and Lesbian Movement*. "Though fascism was defeated in Germany, a reactionary coalition had mobilized in the United States, reaching its height in the early 1950s with the prosecutorial activities of Senator Joseph McCarthy and the U.S. House Committee on Un-American Activities."

And "in the glow of postwar optimism that illuminated the familism of the late 1940s and 1950s, journalists and social scientists alike rekindled the disdain for the unmarried person that had always smoldered beneath the surface of American culture," says the insightful book *The Age of the Bachelor*, which focuses on the phenomenon of single men migrating to urban centers in the late nineteenth century, and how social and economic forces ultimately squashed the bachelor culture that developed. It points to the 1949 volume *Why Are You Single?*, which "typified the prevailing attitude [of that time] among medical experts, social scientists, and the clergy: the unmarried state was unnatural and socially dysfunctional."

Thus the antihomosexual campaigns of the 1950s were part of a larger attempt to return sexual and gender norms back to a marriage-oriented society, with stay-at-home moms who not only kept the home domestic but their men as well. The sexual deviant was an example of what *not* to be, shaping the mold of what it meant to be a *normal* man or woman, while at the same time cranking up the perception of dysfunction on those who remained outside the traditional family structure.

It was an era of "traditional" values, where even nonsexual intimacies between men became stigmatized as a result of homo-paranoia.

"As long as friendship was something important, was socially accepted, nobody realized men had sex together," writes Michel Foucault. "The disappearance of friendship as a social relation and the declaration of homosexuality as a social/political/medical problem are the same process."

As homosexuality was pushed more and more into the public psyche, the more entrenched it became as a dangerous pathology, as *the* sign, along with communism, of inversion or perversion. And while the Kinsey Report demonstrated that flamboyance was not a necessary indicator for homosexuality, the single state *was* a telltale sign for this "dysfunction." The way men interacted started to change. Psychiatry began not only to probe men's sexual activities but to link emotional attachments betweem members of the same sex as an inclination toward homosexuality. Thus, even signs of nonphysical intimacy (i.e., friendship) became signs of illness in need of treatment.

Such policies, coupled with a postwar drive for stability, seemed to be having the desired effect. According to Peter J. Stein in his 1976 book *Single,* by the mid-1950s couples were entering marriage at the youngest ages on record.

And while attitudes toward singles did soften in the '60s, in *The Mating Trade*, John Goodwin sums up the anti-singles conspiracy that played out, and which can still be felt today.

"In modern America," he writes "the position of singles of both genders was oddly ambiguous. They enjoyed considerable freedom and were not subjected to any official discrimination. Yet society treated them as people somehow outside the national norm . . . made to feel downright alien during the years of the great Togetherness Cult, a mania birthed jointly by Madison Avenue and Hollywood, which regarded singleness as akin to halitosis."

This of course is a key part of the conspiracy. Anti-singleness is not written into law, except perhaps in tax breaks for married couples, and through work-related health benefits. The pressures are more social, starting from childhood, and increasing into adulthood, carrying on with Mom asking "So, are you seeing anyone?"

Fortunately, many gay men are saying fuck it.

Saying No to the Conspiracy

"It's emotional blackmail," says award-winning author Wayson Choy, who is more than familiar with the push to pair on gay men. "There's a lot of pressure. You might as well be Chinese."

Choy knows this all too well. In the old days Chinese men could have many women, and heritage was everything, he tells me. "We have over a hundred terms for family linear relationships." Sons were ranked according to a complicated series of numerical assignations, such as number two son of number three concubine.

"There would be particular ways to state that and . . . it could be very complex. It was a life or death matter if someone was misnumbered or misnamed."

Choy managed to escape a lot of the Chinese cultural pressure to marry by moving away from Vancouver's Chinatown in the '60s. But when he returned as a visitor to family events, the now sixty-six-year-old notes, "Quite frankly many of them could see the obvious. 'He's not going to get married, let's just get with this, but does he have anybody?' I remember one or two of my family members would say to me 'well you should have somebody you know, it doesn't matter who.' But I thought *my god, I have the world! I have just the closest friends I could imagine having.*"

And yet it's almost as if there's a tribe of Stepford Wives across North America, conspiring to get everyone, including gay men, into a relationship. In the remake of the movie, there's even a gay duo. They're accepted as long as they are masculine, Republican, and in a couple. "Gay and single is good" has no place in this world, because "single is good" has no place here either, which creates an odd inner tension. On the one hand it's wonderful to have a greater level of gay acceptance. On the other it means gay singles come under the same scrutiny as straight singles, and face the same rejection on that level.

That doesn't mean Choy isn't appreciative of the gains in gay visibility, both within heterosexual culture as a whole and for Asian queer culture in particular, without which his biological relatives might not even ask him about his emotional life. He could certainly see how far behind Canada was when he first came out and would visit San Francisco in the '70s, which he describes as an American Asian city. He says gay Asian groups there were ahead of their time and he's glad to see other cities catching up. He can't help but reminisce as he thinks back to those days.

"I grew up in the age of James Dean. You'd have to dust that off to remember. He was an ideal for me. A preconscious ideal really. . . . You have to remember that in my days, the dark ages, homosexuality was hardly talked about except in very negative ways. . . . You were evil, you're a pervert, you're a degenerate, and none of those things c'est moi!"

He's smiling and jovial as he says this, but a lingering resentment creeps into his tone as the topic turns to the state of his singlehood, and how others react to it. As he put it, there are no trucks driving on his highway anymore, and though that can always change, he'd like it if those around him would stop asking him about it.

"People will say out of the blue you must be so happy with whoever you're with, you're such a nice person. When I say I don't have anybody . . ." His shoulders heave as he lets go a big sigh in imitation of their reaction. "Oh, you have to," they say. "If they like you, part of the way they mean well is to wish you with somebody as lovely as you."

"Which is a wonderful sentiment," I offer.

"Which is a *faked* sentiment, because they're not paying

attention to who I am. I'll tell you what it's like. When people say to a friend of mine, *oh I don't even think of you as being black,* she replies: *You better honey. You see what I am.* When somebody looks at you as a person and then thinks you need something, they don't actually see you when you're quite willing to be there with them as is. And it's a blackmailing question, its unconscious, but well-meaning people pave the way to hell. . . . Better they should say you must have a lot of friends because you're just such a neat person. Not, poor thing, are you such a good person and lonely, too? It's like saying I don't see who you are. Do you have a sign that says *available? Desperate?*"

Choy's characterization sums it up: there really is a conspiracy of Stepford Wives, trying to pressure singles into a couples mold.

"A lot of people surrender to that pressure because they've played the game too long and don't know how to get out of it so they play it destined to fail," says Choy. "It's like you're in a casino and you play this game and here are the rules and the longer you play the more the casino wins until you're broke."

The Hierarchy of Love

So how is it that gays even got dealt in at the poker game? After all, they were once used as a tool of the conspiracy to pressure single men into putting all their chips into marrying women. What changed? The answer lies on the hierarchy of love.

In her seminal 1984 essay "Thinking Sex," anthropologist

Gayle Rubin breaks down a series of social and sexual activities into two opposing categories as they are embraced by mainstream culture:

Good, normal, natural.

Bad, abnormal, unnatural.

Married is better than unmarried. Monogamous is better than promiscuous. In a relationship is better than casual. Straight is better than gay. Put it all together and apply it to relationships and it means Married Straights are better than Coupled Straights are better than Single Straights are better than Gays. Now of course gay couples have moved on up the ladder, while singles linger behind.

I think of the cult hit movie *Muriel's Wedding,* which has found a strong following in the gay world for much more than its Abba soundtrack.

"You're not nothing, Muriel," her friend Rhonda tells her. "Remember how you were in school? You were so quiet you could hardly talk. You were too shy to look at people. Now you're a success, and someone wants to marry you. You're not nothing, Muriel. You've made it."

But made it where?

To the top of the hierarchy of love.

In the 1970s gay culture as a whole recognized that different people needed different things and did not openly buy into the hierarchy. In the 1950s gay couples weren't even on it, except as part of a degenerate mass at the bottom of the barrel to be used to pressure bachelors into marriage.

But I now witness gays buying into the hierarchy of love in places where I'd least expect it, like surfing on m4m4sex.com. As the name implies, the Web site is geared toward men hooking up for sex, not relationships, but lines like "ideally looking for an LTR but willing to mess around in the meanwhile" or "in a relationship; we only play as a couple" have not only become clichés of the new millennium, they set the couple as the primary ideal and other entanglements as secondary compromises.

So what got gays all rah-rah about boyfriends and husbands, and what got homo-accepting straights equally excited about this concept? In other words, how did gay couplehood start moving on up in the hierarchy, leaving gay singles at the bottom?

Gay Couples Clamber Up the Ladder of Love

To answer these questions I pull open the drawer of my filing cabinet. I feel like Mulder sans Scully, flipping through the pieces that will help me solve the puzzle of my own *X-Files*. Photocopies lie cocooned within dark green hanging folders and handwritten labels poke up as if they were placards at a protest.

"Gay Marriage 1990s."

"Relationships 1980s."

"The Scene 1970s."

My fingers dance across these dangling pods of haphazardly organized fragments of gay love and loss. My eyes forage ahead, falling on the file I'm looking for, and my fingers leapfrog to catch up, latching onto the folder and jerking it free from the surrounding mass.

"Newfound Maturity," it reads.

Inside the folder is the *Newsweek* from August 8, 1983. On the cover is a man with a mustache, wearing a loosened tie and a dress jacket with a triangle pinned to the lapel. He leans his head on the shoulder of a guy in a jean jacket. Jean Jacket Guy has an arm wrapped around Mr. Mustache's shoulder, and another hand firmly clasping the inside of Mustache's closest arm.

"Gay America," it reads. "Sex, Politics and the Impact of AIDS."

The article inside is titled: "Gay America in Transition. A turning point has been reached, and AIDS may mean the party is over."

It begins with a description of the Hothouse, described as "legendary in gay San Francisco . . . a four-story, 10,000 square foot pleasure palace." Amid a description of chains and harnesses, the article hones in on the Hothouse's centerpiece: a giant tire swing, "boyish and innocent amid the ominous clutter of leather restraining devices."

It's pegged as symbolic of what the article describes as a "therapeutic playpen" in the eyes of owner Louis Gaspar. He's quoted as calling it "a place where gay men could live out their adolescence, sexually and playfully, because so many of us never got through that phase."

But those days, it would seem, and the hierarchy itself, would never be the same again.

Within the gay community, a deadly sexually transmitted disease made promiscuity less appealing, particularly as early AIDS education pushed gays to limit their partners. Gay and single was not looking so good anymore. And there were more pressing concerns than leveling the institution of hierarchical love.

The "in-laws" were coming.

Queers Fight to Get on the Hierarchy

The 1980s fight to win gay rights veered away from sexual ideologies and focused on immediate concerns, such as getting access to life-prolonging drugs, and legal recognition for gay couples. Gay couples could no longer afford not to be on the hierarchy, illusory or not, if they were to have any kind of humane legal consideration in the face of laws that were tailored to a pair-bonded society.

As a literal case of life and death, the AIDS crisis forced queer activist groups into new arenas with greater urgency, taking on battles that might otherwise have remained on the backburner.

"The issues that AIDS raised were first of all cases involving hospitals and partners of people with AIDS and having access to them . . . and recognizing the partner as a decision maker in medical issues," Urvashi Vaid tells me. Vaid is an attorney, community organizer, and writer whose work in social justice organizations spans more than twenty-five years. She's worked at the global social justice group the Ford Foundation since 2001, and the previous fifteen years she worked for the National Gay and Lesbian Task Force, the oldest national GLBT civil rights organization in the United States. When it came to visiting the sick and the dying, activists urged health officials to recognize that many gay men looked upon friends and lovers as primary family.

"Other cases involved funerals, would a partner be involved . . . and what happens to a rent controlled apartment when a lover dies," says Vaid. Belongings were also at risk. Families could, and did, cart away possessions after not even speaking to their deceased son or sibling for years, leaving his lover with nothing.

"The epidemic made our lives more visible to government and medical providers and all sorts of businesses," says Vaid. "We were able to talk about the family that we had, and the lack of recognition we had. The tragedy and trauma made vivid the need for some kind of recognition in particular situations."

To get that recognition required raising gay couples onto the hierarchy of love to be on par with straight couples, or at the very least, narrowing the legal gap between the two so that gay couples were not completely at the mercy of a system designed for straight pairings.

Politically, queers were also being hit by the barrage of Anita Bryant and her save the children crusade.

Vaid continues, "Remember the right wing had a family values rhetoric starting in the '70s with the so-called Moral

Majority and the opposition to the local gay rights laws that were passed. By the '80s the whole family values rhetoric generated a response from gays. We have families. How dare you try to take us out of that!"

A New Maturity

The sentiment Urvashi Vaid expresses, of not wanting to be left out of society, was another key motivator in the fight by gays to get onto the hierarchy, a flame that was also fanned by the AIDS epidemic.

"What exactly, after all, did a third of a million Americans die for? If not for their fundamental equality, then what?" asks agent provocateur Andrew Sullivan in *Love Undetectable: Notes on Friendship, Sex, and Survival.* His drive to have same-sex love fully recognized was a direct result of the impact of AIDS on the emotional landscape of gay men's lives.

"When people ask me why I became obsessed with the issue of marriage during the plague, I can only respond by saying that it had everything to do with this," he writes.

"Before the plague, we had felt content to think of it as merely the temporary occasions of desire snatched in the shadows, or the fleeting moments of cultural rebellion we had come to mistake for progress, or simply the quiet calm of an unexpected, public embrace," writes Sullivan. "But as the plague grew, the depth of the experience intimated a different depth of liberation. It was not enough any longer to experience love or to capture it. It was necessary to own it, and to

have the love acknowledged. . . . Acknowledgment is enfran-
chisement, as every heterosexual spouse understands. So as the
world was forced to acknowledge the reality of our deaths, we
dared dream it could acknowledge the reality of our lives."

His hopes were not utterly in vain.

The question of where gays were going to fit in the new
order was going to have to be tackled at some point. After all,
as Andrew Sullivan indicates, straights were being forced to
acknowledge gays in ways that they didn't have to before.

Keep in mind that despite popular mythology, the closet
door wasn't entirely blown open after the Stonewall Riots. The
freedom of the '70s was bought at a cost long before AIDS
became the ultimate spoilsport. As that 1983 *Newsweek* article
put it, there was "a mutual accommodation between straights
and gays, the gays agreeing not to flaunt their homosexuality
and the straights agreeing not to notice it."

The result, particularly in larger cities like LA and New
York, were separate, if not quite secret, societies. Gays who
were out in Chelsea were not necessarily so with family and
colleagues. People might know, but no one talked about it.
AIDS altered that, at least within the white community. The
illnesses and deaths were not things that could be hidden,
forcing many gay men into the public eye who might otherwise have remained under the radar in work and family life,
even while flaming it up in their ghettos.

As long as homosexual remained separate, the hierarchy of
love could play off them as lesser and "other." There was also

a perception of carefree freedom from responsibility that "justified" denying gays full equality and adult status. But AIDS permanently transformed the unspoken terms of acceptance between gays and straights, and a policy of don't ask don't tell within the larger culture could not sustain itself.

"The epidemic changed that," says Vaid. "AIDS brought visibility all over the country, because [gay] people were living all over the country and were dying, including in Nebraska. . . . Suddenly it confronted people and it was constant. It was your neighbor's son. The friend you went to school with."

As Sullivan points out, it was oddly in death that gay men gained a certain level of equality. The secretive freedom and power of gay men were perceived to have melted away. "Death, it turned out, was a powerfully universalizing experience. . . . From being powerful subversives, they were now dying sons."

If the conspiracy were a living, breathing entity, I imagine it would be at home dropping its can of beer while watching all of this on TV, and thinking *shit. Dying SONS? You've got to be fucking kidding me. Jesus H. Christ! I can't use goddamn dying sons in a campaign to guilt singles into getting married. The Christian Right will do its best with their whole wrath of God AIDS-baiting bit, but once Hollywood finally gets its crap together, there's a fucking red-ribbon campaign and a Tom Hanks movie just waiting the fuck to happen. I just know it! God fucking damn it!*

I almost feel like the conspiracy's spin doctors banded together in a late-night emergency session in some secret bunker to grudgingly draft a policy statement to straights and homos alike on the social conditions and rules for adapting to this new era. One way or another, homos were going to reinforce the hierarchy of love, keeping couplehood safely at the top. An eloquent statement of that policy, written in the form of an article, was then printed in *Newsweek*.

"For Gay America, a decade of carefree sexual adventure, a headlong gambol on the far side of the human libido, has all but come to a close. The flag of sexual liberation that had flown as the symbol of the gay movement has been lowered. Caution and responsibility—to oneself, to one's friends, to the larger and still pressing concerns of gay life in America—are now the watchwords of gay liberation, and many homosexuals do not regret it. . . . Virtually to a man, gay leaders speak of a 'new maturity' that is replacing the last decade's mood of pansexual excess."

The conditions for gay grown-up-hood were being set. Couplehood may not have been specifically mentioned, but it was just a matter of time. This is, after all, one of the fundamental institutions of being a grown-up. The other of course is economic success.

The Pink Dollar Comes of Age

As sociologist Gary Kinsman points out, there was a real economic transformation of the gay scene following the sexploration of the '70s. There emerged a commercial ghetto in the

'80s and '90s, accompanied (or perhaps fuelled) by an explosion of what's now perceived as the most "legitimate" part of queer society—the gay middle class.

"In the early '70s we would have emphasized our differences and didn't want to buy into that heterosexual mythology," says Kinsman. "There's been a real transformation. . . . If you're gay middle class and want to be accepted in the broader society, you want to adopt those middle class norms which revolve around family and marriage. The landscape's been reshaped."

Queer singledom was losing steam while coupled respectability, with the privileges and responsibilities that entailed, gained more momentum.

Writing about the late '70s and early '80s in *The Case for Same-Sex Marriage,* William N. Eskridge Jr. says that gay marriage "languished in a generational purgatory." He says this cohort of out gays was "ambivalent about marriage." But as the '80s progressed there was a "stealthy revival" of the push for legalized gay marriage, motivated by an aging gay and lesbian population. "Queer boomers" were "making more money than love, and settling down with partners. The guppie (gay urban professional) with a partner and a Porsche was replacing the free love advocate with a placard and a toke."

As these middle-class gays entered the height of their spending power, they were also entering their thirties and were naturally inclined to slow down. Travel, gym memberships, homes, and expensive electronics became visible priorities.

Sex as a lifestyle was on the decline, in part because it just wasn't economically feasible for the upwardly mobile gay man. Longtime activist and trained economist Jeffrey Escoffier once published a newsletter entitled *Gay People in the Labor Force* as he tried to figure out where he fit into the workforce as an openly gay man.

He says that it used to be that "you'd go to San Francisco, you'd work as a waiter or in a bar, you'd have sex and drugs all the time, and if you got fired, you'd get another short-term job. You did not go to San Francisco to pursue a career. You did it to explore sex." But he says that's not so feasible anymore. "San Francisco's too expensive. Where are you going to go? Hoboken? Even Hoboken's too expensive. It's difficult to live outside the global economy."

And even socially things have changed. Once, he says, nobody would question you if you were to "disappear for five years," work a crappy job, and explore your sexuality. Who does that anymore? Who would look up to you if you did?

As Escoffier concludes: "You can't be fucking around the way you could in the '70s."

The New Gay Order

It would seem the article in *Newsweek* claiming a newfound maturity in the gay world was as much prophecy as propaganda. "The long escape into hedonism has most of all been a reckless diversion of Gay America's energies—energies that must now be directed into winning political gains, and winning

[the] hearts and minds of men and women who, in many communities, live right next door."

This philosophy, and that of a new maturity, was taken very seriously by some of the most outspoken proponents of gay marriage in a fight that would gain strength in the 1990s. Success for gay rights increased over the years as litigation focused on the legal and economic benefits denied queer couples, shifting the debate away from questions of reproduction and religion and in fact sex altogether. And step by step, equality *is* being gained, to the point where same-sex marriage is now legal in many countries. In the United States, it is legal only in Massachusetts, but in several other states unmarried couples are now given some of the rights granted to those in traditional unions.

Unfortunately, it is equality in a system that is in and of itself inequitable, as straight singles have long known.

Long live the conspiracy.

3. Love Is Not a Hierarchy, Even if Gay Progress Means Pretending It Is

Being gay and single is the new smoking. . . . It won't be socially acceptable anymore, and you will have to go outside.

—Paul Rudnick, playwright
New York Times, March 7, 2004

S O THERE'S A CONSPIRACY.

The hierarchy of love is its prime tool, one that first *really* smacked me on the ass back in my midteens. I was flipping through a current affairs magazine when my eyes flashed over a page with an item in the bottom corner about physique maestro Bob Paris.

This man whose image inspired more of my pubescent orgasms than I could recall, wet dreams included, had not only come out, he was married to a gorgeous hunk of a man, a fitness model no less.

It was the dream.

But could Mr. Universe Bob Paris really be into sucking cock? It just seemed too good to be true. As a gawky teenager whose cyst-covered back was finally in remission thanks to the intense oral acne medication Accutane, this gay story of my bodybuilding hero gave me hope.

It may seem cheesy now, safe as I am, perched in my high-rise condo, but back then, as the Accutane shrank my oil glands, making my lips peel constantly and forcing me to smear them with Vaseline every hour or two (prompting more than one joke from my classmates), the article showed me something beyond that present.

I desperately tried to track down the original article, from *Ironman* magazine, where he came out, but to no avail. Now, more than a decade and a half later, long after the article fell off my radar, I walk into the Canadian Lesbian & Gay Archives and ask one of the volunteers for the Bob Paris file.

The folder is handed to me two minutes later, and without even a drum roll in my head, I flip it open. And voila. There he is, on the cover of *Ironman*, shirtless and holding a bike over one shoulder, with the understated words: "Bob Paris Is True to Himself," giving no indication of the coming out that unfolds within its glossy pages. Perhaps then it's appropriate that as I read through the interview, my bright pink highlighter acting like a divining rod, I find myself not so concerned with the details of his coming out so much as I'm drawn to the tidbits about his "marriage."

The first time he and Rod Jackson met at a gym, he tells journalist Lonnie Teper, "BAM. We both knew we were destined to spend the rest of our lives together."

"[We] are a normal married couple," he insists. "My moral standards are as high as anyone else's. We don't sleep around. We have a wonderful dog Samantha, and a blue and gold macaw named Barney who we dote on as our children. . . . I want people to realize I am a gay, married man. . . . I want it to be known that I'm not a single man, and I don't want to have to live the lie that I am."

I feel an edge in me as I read this, like an X-Acto blade sliding out. What slaps me is him putting "normal" and "married" side by side. "I want it to be known that I'm not a single man" is acid backwash. Intellectually I know he's not putting down singles with these statements, that he's simply stating the truth of his own situation at the time. As a teen I would've drunk this up, so it's telling how defensive I've become more than a decade later. We've gone from him hiding his relationship, to gay singles apologizing and feeling somehow like we have to justify not having one.

Neither is an acceptable scenario.

The Other Side of Gay Marriage

Unfortunately, with a de facto policy of don't ask don't tell permeating too many communities and households when it comes to gay love, queer couples clambering the hierarchy will likely continue to be the path of choice for gaining equal rights. If nothing else, it gives us all more visibility. But before buying into our own pair-bonded hype by believing there is something wrong with singles, just remember the "other side of gay marriage," as a 1996 issue of the *Advocate* put it.

On the cover is Paris. He's still handsome and well built, stretching his clothes to the max, but the youthful smiling shots from past glossies have been supplanted by more somber pictorials. He's got a few gray hairs. Rod is nowhere to be seen. The marriage cracked under a variety of strains, including the limelight they both found and placed themselves in. Some took satisfaction in the demise of a marriage between two such physical beauties, and never felt they truly represented the community in that respect. The current slew of media images of average- and below-average-looking gays and lesbians getting married bears that out.

The reality is not quite as I'd fantasized as I jerked off to *Muscle&Fitness* and Herb Ritz black-and-white photos. My intention is not to attack Paris (though it could easily be interpreted as such). In his book *Generation Queer* he talks about being "written off as irrelevant" by other queers because of how he looked and because he came into his activism out of bodybuilding. I don't want to add to that sense of scorn. To be clear, he was the first gay person I ever knew, even though we have to this day never met. To a closeted teenager it meant a lot to see this icon come out. When I read that he and his husband of the time had split, I was sad and distressed. After his marriage ended he writes that he worked hard not to become one who "sneers" at relationships.

Throughout this book I have striven to follow his lead. But the idea of couplehood as *the* route to fulfillment, as a condition of entering into "maturity," and as the love of all loves, must be challenged, as does the raw emotion of marriage ceremonies themselves. We cannot simply give into this extortion of the heart, for there remains a difference between love as a social policy and how love plays itself out in real life. Marriage is not the culmination of the ultimate love for everybody, even if, for gay rights to move forward, we must sometimes pretend it is. But for our own sake and within our own communities we must also stop and acknowledge how love actually plays out in the lives of many gay men.

Friendships as Rite of Passage

"We discovered we wanted different things," my friend and Canadian Leatherman 2004 Paul Ciantar says to me over lunch one day, telling me about one of his ex-boyfriends. I listen to what is a common tale. "I still love him. I know he still loves me. He still buys me birthday presents. His partner of one and a half years is a great guy, we get along fine. We're adult enough that we realized that if we stuck it out for the house and stuff we'll wind up hating each other and resenting one another, and we didn't want that."

There is the usual pride in his voice that I often hear from ex-boyfriends who've "worked it out," *not* by staying lovers but by remaining friends, as if it were a reflection of their own ability to negotiate the rocky waters that can separate an ended love relationship from a potentially great friendship.

For gay men, I really do believe entering into friendship is a rite of passage, one that can take many shapes, and more than marriage or a boyfriend is a sign of entering into our emotional maturity.

Consider Queer as Folk Syndrome (named by me after the original British TV show, which inspired the longer running American series). The story spins around two gay best friends, one of whom is in love with the other. They are forced to negotiate this treacherous territory, and come through as companions in the life.

In the movie *Brother to Brother,* which flashes back between contemporary gay black culture and the Harlem Renaissance, we see another twist on QAF Syndrome play out between nineteen-year-old Perry and the aging character of gay black writer Bruce Nugent.

Perry's been kicked out of his house for being gay and is reeling from the experience, while also grappling with his attraction to a sexually confused schoolmate, Jim.

"My whole idea with this relationship with Jim and also Bruce is that Perry was searching for this idea of a mate and thinking that Jim would fulfill it. And there was this fundamental lack of trust that prevented it from evolving," writer/director Rodney Evans explains to me from his home in Brooklyn. "What Perry was looking for from Jim he ultimately gets from Bruce in this nonsexual but intimate and profound friendship. He was looking for this sexual, romantic relationship but finds something that's equally as important and life changing in this elderly figure hovering around the story and around his life."

For the character of Bruce there is a flip side to all this. Bruce is in his elderly years yet very much remains a sexualized, flirtatious, wise, and witty human being. There is a physical longing for Perry, but it is clear that's not going to go anywhere. Still, there is something else for him in this scenario.

"Bruce is an older artist, struggling to stay inspired as an older artist, and this inspiration comes from Perry. Seeing this younger version of himself sparks a creative spirit in him that he has longed for and lost touch with. He's also interested in the fact that this kid is so taken with him, and deems his life important and is interested in hearing about it. Both characters are in the process of feeling each other out, and if they can trust one another, then I think the friendship has a huge transformative effect on both of them."

Tricks, Lovers, and Exes

These are the unacknowledged rites of passage that most gay men involved in the culture must go through to reach emotional adulthood, not in finding romantic love but in finding platonic love beyond it, for almost all of us sooner or later fall for a friend we can never have "in that way," or remain friends with an ex, or find the guiding love of a mentor, or become enchanted with someone who is much too young to be a boyfriend but still has much to offer as a friend.

And often that's not where the story ends but rather gets off to an unlikely beginning. It might *end* a boyfriendship rather than ending *with* one.

But while "finding" love in the form of a boyfriend is revered, we fail to recognize that it is by navigating the turbulent waters of desire *un*returned that many queer boys lead themselves to the shores of emotional adulthood, often greeted by sailors of friendship with whom we will never have sex with, or not anymore, or not within the context of the relationship we might have once envisioned.

This is a rite without ceremony that far more of us go through than get married, and for many of us gay singles at least, of far more use, as we continue to wade through strange waters where it's often unclear whether we may touch or not, if someone's available or not, if we're flirting or if we're *flirting*, if we're going to make love or fuck around or just hang out.

As Michael Warner points out in his provocative 1999 book *The Trouble with Normal* (which argues against same-sex marriage), we have no specific words for how special many of these relationships remain or become to us.

"Between tricks and lovers and exes and friends and fuck

buddies and bar friends and bar friends' tricks and tricks' bar friends and gal pals and companions 'in the life,' queers have an astonishing range of intimacies. Most have no labels. Most receive no public recognition. Many of these relations are difficult because the rules have to be invented as we go along. Often desire and unease add to their intensity, and their unpredictability. They can be complex and bewildering, in a way that arouses fear among many gay people, and tremendous resistance and resentment from many straight people. Who among us would give them up?"

Not many.

In a survey by Peter Nardi and Drury Sherrod ("Friendships in the lives of gay men and lesbians," 1994), out of 161 gay men, about 82 percent of them said they had a gay or bisexual male best friend. In referring to this study in the collection of writing *Men's Friendships*, Nardi states "almost 80% of the gay men said they were attracted to their best friend in the past, and 52% continue to be attracted to him. Around 60% said they had sex with their best friend in the past, and 20% continue do so. About 57% were in love with their best friend in the past, and 48% still are. . . . Approximately 20% of the gay men also said their current best friend is an ex-lover."

Saying that the highest of love is between a man and a woman and enshrining it in laws does not make it so. Neither does doing the same for a man and a man. Nor does marriage even mean two people are in love or will stay in love.

Love is too rich, and at times shifting, for any such hierarchy to accommodate. It's not likely that straights as a whole are going to get this. In fact there are still lots of straights who don't "get" homosexuality in general. And while paradoxically it might be in these conservative arenas that gay marriage is most fiercely reviled, it is also in these arenas where gay progress will most likely follow a couple's model.

I doubt lingo like "QAF Syndrome" and "friendship as rite of passage" is going to catch on in the straight world, particularly not in the most conservative of enclaves. Romantic pair-bonding, on the other hand, is familiar territory. Even if gays put a different and at times uncomfortable spin on couple-hood, it's still a model that conservatives can relate to, and thus one that can be exploited to further gay rights, even if it doesn't reflect how a lot of gay men are living their lives.

Love as a PR Tool

"I think there's an interesting dichotomy between the public conservative rhetoric around gay marriage and how Republicans actually relate to gay couples," says Patrick Guerriero of the gay Republican group the Log Cabin Republicans. As the organization's president, Guerriero is in the unique position of meeting and mingling with some of the most conservative people in the United States, and he's certainly seen Republicans fight to maintain the legal status quo of straight unions at the top of the hierarchy of love. It was during his first three years at Log Cabin's helm, beginning in 2003, that the culture war over gay marriage really broke out, from the U.S. Supreme Court forcing Texas to revoke its sodomy laws to the slew of cities issuing marriage licenses to queer couples.

"Things were boiling right at the time that I took over," he says.

He was shocked and angered by the proposed amendment to the U.S. Constitution that would have defined marriage as being between a man and a woman, and it was the first time in the organization's twenty-seven-year history that it did not support a Republican president. But for all this, he says there's a big difference between a conservative at the podium and the same conservative at a cocktail party. Outside the court of public opinion, the hierarchy is not so easy to maintain.

"It's easier for [straight] people struggling with this issue to be at a dinner party with a gay couple than respond to a floor debate on gay marriage. Dinner parties, cocktail parties, gays living in the neighborhood, being at a political meeting together, that changes things."

He's experienced this apparent paradox firsthand, all the way up to the Oval Office, meeting President Bush during a Christmas party.

"I have a boyfriend, but he was not with me at that event. But the president obviously knows I'm gay because of the beautiful pink dress that I wear to the White House." Joking aside, Guerriero says that although the president's gay-related policies have frustrated him, he says socially Bush is very gracious.

And the reverse plays out similarly, when some of the most conservative politicians in the United States attend the Log

Cabin's annual convention as keynote speakers and see queer couples holding hands and being affectionate.

"The introduction of boyfriends and relationships to conservative Republicans is both fascinating and transforming," he says. "It's like a coming out process for them. The neatest way to do it is have the gay or lesbian couple that's been together twenty-five years look exactly like people in legislative office."

But Guerriero admits the experience can be more than a little surreal.

"You're in the company of folks who may have recently publicly said things that marginalize your family, yet they're as gracious as anyone else in the company of you and your boyfriend. . . . George Bush and Barbara Bush are particularly gracious around gay couples. . . . It's a very odd experience, but it's how you change people's hearts and minds. It personalizes it in a way that issues don't. In some ways it is gay partners or boyfriends in the company of people who may have been anti-gay who break the stereotypes. I think the far right reaction to gay and lesbian folk is being transformed by gay relationships."

In other words, if single is the new gay in progressive environments, then gay couplehood is the new visibility in conservative ones. Seeing and treating the love of a gay couple as less than the love of a straight couple becomes more difficult, face to face, in venues where one must not cause a scene, as well it should, because love is *not* a hierarchy. Love is just love.

In the past, Guerriero says, marginalizing gays was easier when "it was always the neighbor who had a roommate or the uncle who came to Thanksgiving dinner alone, or the person who brought his friend to family reunions. As that shifts to the couple, it really does change the framework for a lot of people, including a lot of conservative people."

So people "get it" on some level, that love manifests in different ways. The ripple effect emanates as far up the chain of command as Vice President Dick Cheney himself.

Same-sex marriage is the "only policy that he publicly disagreed with the President on because his daughter and her girlfriend are at the White House having dinner. That single relationship allows the Vice President to publicly disagree only once. For that to happen at that level you melt it down and see how it will play out in a decade or two."

What Guerriero foresees is a generation of gay and lesbian young people who will "just expect to get married."

This is a pity, as it means that whatever progress gays are making, it is at the cost of recognizing that love takes many shapes. And I worry when I hear certain gay marriage activists who actually seem to believe their own hype, to the point where they think that love actually *is* a hierarchy, that some loves *are* better than others, and that couplehood, particularly as it's canonized by marriage, is *the* sign of gay maturity. This completely ignores that homosexual behavior was once popularly viewed as a phase some youths might go through before "growing up" and into heterosexuality. That was the sign of gay maturity: giving up cock. I also get the sense that some same-sex marriage activists really believe the institution of marriage is right for *everyone* and that the institution *should* be on top, rather than simply capitalizing on the fact that it's legally treated as such.

Love as a Social Policy

An "educational guide" put out by the Lambda Legal Defense and Education Fund is a perfect example. The group was formed in 1973 and now has offices in New York, Los Angeles, Chicago, Atlanta, and Dallas. The group boasts a number of breakthrough legal actions over the years, from obtaining full visitation rights for a gay father, to successfully challenging a series of antisodomy laws in the United States, to helping to pressure the makers of AZT to lower their prices. Now it is at the forefront of the gay marriage movement in the United States. Lambda Legal, along with Marriage Equality California, put out *Roadmap to Equality: A Freedom to Marry Educational Guide*.

The guide raises some good points, which are mirrored on Lambda's Web site, that much like separate-but-equal racial laws that have now been abolished, marriage is marriage, and calling gay unions anything else is discriminatory.

But other arguments it presents enter dodgier territory. It openly states that "married couples are held in greater esteem than unmarried couples because of the commitment they have made in a serious, public, legally enforceable manner," using this as an argument in favor of gay marriage rather than as a challenge to the hierarchy created by this institution. I don't have a problem with gay marriage per se, and for many years I had my swanky tuxedo fantasies of walking down the aisle with the hunk of my life, I mean the love of my life, at my side. It's been years since I've pictured such an image, and now, as a single gay man I do take issue with some of the arguments being used to fight for gay matrimony.

Such as the "psychological consequences" of treating gay couples like "second-class citizens" (no mention of the psychological consequences of treating singles as third class). Or the statement that by not allowing us to marry we are kept "in a state of permanent adolescence."

And it is not just one "educational guide" promoting these ideas.

William Eskridge unabashedly sums up this thesis in the subtitle of his book, *The Case for Same-Sex Marriage: From Sexual Liberty to Civilized Commitment*. He argues that marriage "civilizes" gays and points out that the word can mean "integrate into the law and customs of society." But as he makes explicit, he's also using the word in its other, more "provocative" sense, to "tame" or "domesticate": "To the extent that males in our culture have been more sexually venturesome (more in need of civilizing) . . . same-sex marriage could be a particularly useful commitment device for gay and bisexual men."

The ramifications for gay singles seem both frosty and puritanical, and it sounds an awful lot like the idea that if only a homo found the right woman, she'd set him straight, literally and figuratively, onto the mature path of hetero-normative family marriage and reproduction. She would, in essence, civilize the gender outlaw into a member of society.

"Whatever gravity gay life may have lacked in the disco seventies it acquired in the health crisis of the eighties," Eskridge goes on to say. "What it lost in youth and innocence it gained in dignity."

Does this then mean that if I'm never coupled, let alone married, that I am undignified? That I am somehow "less" than those who are in relationships? And those who are in gay couples but not married, with no intention of getting married, are less than those who have "committed" through a ceremony? These arguments are based not on equality but on the same inequality that has long plagued straight singles. It also ignores a 40 to 50 percent divorce rate among heterosexual couples, not to mention those who remain in loveless marriages, slowly suffocating.

And yet as we join our solo straight brethren, single homos are like a caravan of camels with valise after valise of extra baggage, stumbling through the Sahara, hoping to find an oasis.

I am, after all, an immature faggot whose heart and cock have no home. And so this is my stigma, my brand, the prefix *single* as much a part of my public identity as the designation gay. My brief reprieve from relationship pressure after coming out has been sucked into this vacuum, and I have been splattered onto the very bottom of the social ladder.

What This Means for Gay Singles

Jonathan Rauch, author of *Gay Marriage: Why It Is Good for Gays, Good for Straights, and Good for America,* sums up the impact on gay singles in his essay, "For Better or Worse," which appeared in the *New Republic,* one of America's most influential journals of politics and opinion.

"If marriage is to work it cannot be merely a 'lifestyle option.' It must be privileged," he says. "It must be understood to be better, on average, than other ways of living. Not mandatory, not good where everything else is bad, but better: a general norm, rather than a personal taste."

Rauch argues that "if gay marriage is recognized, single gay people over a certain age should not be surprised when they are disapproved or pitied. That is a vital part of what makes marriage work. It's stigma as social policy."

So how do I reconcile this with what Log Cabin Republican Patrick Guerriero says next?

"I think that it's gay couples coming out in neighborhoods, political life, and churches that will move progress faster than many would believe today," he tells me.

Hearing these words, I have to be honest. Whatever else I might say about the impact of gay marriage on the stigma of gay singlehood, there's still a part of me that is proud to be living in Canada because same-sex marriage is legal here. When it comes to the hierarchy of love we are equal about our inequality. And to be fair, in 2005 the Supreme Court of Canada ruled that swingers clubs (which allow group sex and partner swapping) don't harm society, effectively protecting bathhouses. These are both major steps forward for those who believe in social and sexual liberty.

Clearly, we don't have to totally buy into the myth that there is a set way to love for gay rights to move forward, and interestingly it was in fact straight swingers clubs that were fighting for the right to operate. There is still, of course, a ways to go, and not just in terms of Republicans altering their antigay public rhetoric to mirror their social etiquette. Even face to face, the social grace only extends so far.

Patrick Guerriero has had many gay-friendly experiences with people who have publicly denounced gay marriage, but there's a limit. While there are plenty of gay men who've been "the single guy" at the Republican cocktail party, he doesn't see a rush of conservatives trying to set them up with other eligible bachelors or inquiring about their emotional lives.

"Conservatives don't go there," says Guerriero. "They're not into gay matchmaking at this stage."

The Future of Gay Acceptance

Guerriero sums up the recurring theme of this chapter. Gay matchmaking would be progress. On the other hand, it also creates a lot of pressure and expectation to be coupled. So until the conspiracy is completely overthrown (good luck), gay progress and relationship pressure are likely to continue going hand in hand.

For example, while the Republican Party may be the dominant conservative voice in the United States, it is by no means the only one, nor even necessarily the benchmark on antihomosexual ideologies. Some feel that Guerriero's more positive experiences do not hold true for a vast number of people in the United States and the world, and that his voice reflects a very specific political and corporate white male power structure.

"White males have the mainstay of that power. . . . What they are comfortable with is what continues, and white male couples can now be seen as the norm," says Daayiee Abdullah, a gay Imam based in Washington, D.C., with an online congregation consisting of just over one thousand Muslims from around the world.

For most gay men of color, he says, things are not quite so nonchalant as Guerriero or my "single is the new gay" catchphrase would imply.

"We have much more to lose economically and from our community," says Abdullah about out gay Muslims.

He's traveled to Muslim nations around the world and says that the elderly single Muslim is often readily recognized as homosexual without consequence, as long as he remains discreet. "When it becomes a public statement is when it becomes frowned upon."

Others who developed a same-sex attachment in a sex-segregated youth might maintain that relationship behind closed doors while also getting married and having kids. "They may be gay, but following societal norms."

It eerily mirrors the "phenomenon" of the so-called "down low," where black men will have a girlfriend or wife-based family but also secretly be having sex with men "on the down low." In his book *Beyond the Down Low: Sex, Lies, and Denial in Black America*, leading commentator on race, politics, and sexuality Keith Boykin details how the story of "the down low" has been blown out of proportion by a salacious media that is all too willing to characterize the libidos of black men as out of control, heaped on top of the stereotype of the hyper-sexual gay or bisexual man. He also points out there are plenty of white guys on the so-called down low.

But Boykin's also quick to criticize the African-American community for perpetuating barriers to gay men of color coming out, pointing to a quiet acceptance of homosexuality within mainstream African-American culture, "as long as it's the occasional individual, and not in a visible relationship."

"I think there's a don't ask don't tell policy within African-American homes and communities. . . . In black churches on any given Sunday you can have a preacher preaching fire and brimstone, but look behind him and there's gays in the choir, ushers . . . and no one tells them they have to leave. It's a paradox."

It's also one of the arenas where future battles for gay rights will likely take place, though probably not through a seven '70s-style sexual liberation rhetoric aimed at overturning the marriage model.

During an unofficial "couple's retreat" to Fire Island, says Boykin, "we were talking a lot about relationships." "There is some pressure in the black gay community to replicate heterosexual relationships. . . . There's an undercurrent and attitude that relationships are good and desirable."

And whether it's legally recognized or not, Daayiee Abdullah says he's performed three same-sex marriages (and eight opposite-sex marriages) in his four years as an Imam. He gets about twelve requests a year from across the United States, around one third of them same sex. The rest are straight. The heteros come to him because they're searching for a more open interpretation of their faith, or because they're more culturally Muslim rather than religiously bound.

There's also been a shift since the events surrounding the attacks on the World Trade Center in how progressive Muslim groups want to be perceived. It catalyzed a reexamination of what it means to be Muslim, from fundamentalists to atheists, and that's opening things up for some queer Muslims.

"If your name was Muhammad, it didn't matter if you were Presbyterian," says Tarek Fatah, one of the founding members of the Muslim Canadian Congress. "I think after September 11 many people were jarred."

A number of Muslim organizations were quick to emphasize that Islam remained a religion of peace and inclusiveness, and worked to steer clear of militant Islam stereotypes. There were those who realized that "strategically, they couldn't be seen as antigay when fighting for rights for Muslims," says Fatah. "If we're fighting for equity we have to fight for universal equity."

This went as far as supporting gay marriage in Canada, when conservative Muslim groups fought against it. Along with women leading Muslim prayers, this is a sign of things to come, at least within Western nations.

For now, Daayiee Abdullah says plans for an online gay Muslim matrimonial site, where Muslims could meet potential long-term partners, have been put on hold. Too many among the target audience were afraid of divulging even the most basic of personal information for the sake of credit checks, worried the information might get out to the larger Muslim community.

"The time is not right for that yet," says Abdullah.

But change is happening, and as in the Republican Party and the black community, it is most likely to progress through a model of couplehood. Most parents who are accepting of their children's queerness are going to want to see them in a long-term partnership.

"I think that holds true no matter what the religion," says Abdullah. "Parents want their children to have a sense of happiness or wholeness."

Ah yes. The parents. Love is not a hierarchy, but sometimes one must pretend it is. If not for the fight for "equal" rights, then for the family's sake.

Love On-Screen

"When I look at you, I feel complete," Rob said to Greg on an episode of the queer reality show *My Fabulous Gay Wedding*, hosted by comic Scott Thompson. In an informal survey, four out of four hardened bitter fags cried while watching it, including yours truly.

It was the wedding vows that did it.

"You have taught me so much about life and love and how to show my true feelings," Rob continued, he and his soon to be husband both dressed in kilts. "It's been the best seven years of my life. And as each day passes I fall deeper and deeper in love with you. We've faced some of life's toughest challenges together and I don't know what I would've done without you by my side. I'm so proud to be standing here with you and I'm so proud for my family for accepting and supporting us with all their hearts. The only regret I have is that you were never able to meet my dad. I know he would've loved you as part of our family. I'm so excited by what lies ahead. I love you."

Instant waterworks.

It was the family stuff that really pushed me over the edge. Marriages, like funerals, are not just about the individual(s) in the limelight, but a gathering of kin to acknowledge one of its own. In the case of marriage, to embrace a new member. Whatever else we might say or do, after years of deception in the closet, deep within many of us still lurks a desire for that ultimate show of acceptance from our families. It's no wonder that PFLAG consistently gets the loudest cheers in Pride parades. Similarly, one gay man tells me about watching one of the first ever filmed depictions of a queer wedding, *Chicks in White Satin*, at the 1993 San Francisco

International Lesbian & Gay Film Festival. Based on his description of the reaction to the film it's not surprising it won that year's Audience Award. "The crowd at the Castro movie theater I saw it in went completely wild—stomping our feet for what seemed like fifteen minutes. I have no idea if that movie lived on in any way. It would be a crying shame if it didn't," he tells me.

And now we've reached the point of gay wedding reality shows. In fact *My Fabulous Gay Wedding* almost rekindled my own fantasies of walking down the aisle to the tune of Dancing Queen. Even host Scott Thompson was not immune, crying his contacts out during one episode. I grew up watching him in the hit comedic sketch show *The Kids in the Hall*. I was a closeted queer boy when it first aired, bonding with my straight brothers over skits rife with gay humor and men playing most of the female roles. I meet with Thompson and ask him about the episode of *My Fabulous Gay Wedding* that brought on his own waterworks.

"They were two young, intelligent, educated, sweet, loving guys. They're like twenty-three years old and they're in love and want to get married, and they were playing *I Will Survive*. Gloria Gaynor." He sighs as he says her name.

"For them it doesn't mean the same thing, and there was a part of me that was really jealous of their life and part of me was very happy that they could do this. They weren't as scarred as my generation. They were much healthier to be honest, emotionally, psychologically. What got me was how many of their friends were not gay. That was very weird for me. In my generation usually your straight friends went by the wayside. This generation is different. These kids came out young. A lot of their friends didn't abandon them. They were all for it, and they weren't forced into the ghetto in that way. The family was very supportive, I just couldn't believe it."

"And the Gloria Gaynor thing, it's kind of pathetic but it just made me think of the way it was for me and my generation. It really was about survival. It wasn't about getting married. I came out in '83, I came out right into AIDS. Our whole thing was will we live? Who's going to die? So to all of a sudden go to let's get married is a very big jump. It got me because I thought we've come so far. . . . All the men that I slept with or had relationships with at the beginning, they're all gone. It was a weird feeling. I was happy for them but also wishing it could've been like that for us."

Listening to this story, and dwelling on my own wonder at guys coming out in high school, I want to end this chapter there. It feels almost sacrilegious not to. But the truth is, that's not where this chapter ends, a fact we oftentimes forget when we watch Big and Carrie happily together on the series finale of *Sex and the City*.

I'm certainly willing to admit that, for some people, couplehood and marriage can be the way to go. But at what point do we stop playing along and pretending this is the way for everyone?

Love in Real Life

"I was the first corporate same-sex spouse in Canada," says Daniel Gelfant, producer of *My Fabulous Gay Wedding*. I'm standing on a ladder in his kitchen. Cardboard boxes fill Gelfant's brand-new two-floor penthouse condo while packing paper litters the floor. He hands me a champagne glass, which I place in the back of the cupboard above his stainless steel fridge. "We used to drink a lot of champagne," he says of his relationship of twelve years, which ended while he was working on the show.

"We married six couples," Gelfant tells me, the crinkling of him unwrapping a vase making me cringe because I know it's going to show up as ambient sound when I play back the tape. Every now and again he pauses to show me one of the treasures accumulated with his partner of more than a decade. "Now this is absolutely necessary," he says, rolling his eyes at himself. "A silver tray that looks like a doily." He sets it on the kitchen counter next to five creamers that could've come out of grandma's china cabinet.

As he unpacks "the detritus of a marriage," as he calls it, he tells me of breakup after breakup among those charged with putting *My Fabulous Gay Wedding* together. "As soon as I started working on it an editor on the series broke up with his boyfriend . . . then a second editor comes into work one day and his eyes were bloodshot and he's a mess. His wife just told him to get out."

They'd just started editing the first wedding story.

"At that moment, I thought *that's two now. I'm next,* says Gelfant." Well, I wasn't next."

A program assistant beat him to it. "Jen and Emma," he says. "I used to call her Bubi, she's so maternal and Jewish. She cried and her mom came over and helped her clean."

He pauses to cut open a box labeled "American art pottery." He unveils a white vase that looks like it's got a seashell growing out of its base. "It's from the '20s," he explains. I guess my own opinion registers on my face because he adds defensively, "I actually like it."

The fifth breakup was "the assistant wedding planner. He's crying all over the place. They bought a condo together. And everyone's all outside smoking and talking about each other's lives."

By show's end, there were six breakups behind the scenes, a seventh not long after, and one of the lesbian couples married on-screen had split by the time the wrap party was held. Less than two year later a second lesbian couple had split. But of course that's not what made it onto TV. In fact, there's much that never made it into the show.

"The American broadcaster wanted us to show gay people in a positive light," says Gelfant of MTV's gay network Logo. "They were very interested in pushing basically gays are just as ordinary as everybody else, so you couldn't put on any couples that spoke of being in a nonmonogamous relationship."

"There was the one couple that spoke about a cheating

incident earlier in their relationship," I counter. "I was impressed by that."

"That was a whole convincing thing to get the network to agree to that. Logo didn't want them cast because they weren't nice enough."

So there is one layer of unreality right there: the selection process that decides which stories get told and who gets to represent couplehood (and singlehood for that matter). By picking only a certain kind of couple, it's easy to create the impression that the love of a couple is tops.

"We're dealing with characters who are sympathetic, who have a mike on, talking about love. How real is that?" asks Gelfant. "And you're not getting them in their everyday lives. You're getting them in selective moments."

And the pressure doesn't just bear on singles. It warps the perceptions of couples as well.

"I remembered hearing the words from the minister and it was the vows and the vows were I vow to blah blah, bring out the best in you always while maintaining my own personal growth. And I thought, I don't think I'm in that kind of relationship anymore."

"But you used to be?" I ask.

"I think I was. But I thought I'm not sure this is bringing out the best in me or that I'm bringing out the best in my partner, and that was the first time I thought, maybe this isn't the person I should be with for the rest of my life. I could actually say that out loud, and then we went to therapy and all that stuff. It was hard, it was really hard. That was the hardest moment I think because the words in those vows were so what the ideal of a marriage was, and that's the thing, that's the problem. You don't live your wedding day. And all I was doing was looking at wedding days. This is not saying I wish I could turn the clock backwards. I'm just saying it was a very intense experience for somebody who was already questioning his relationship. There may have only been six weddings, but we were editing people talking about weddings for a year. I don't think anybody could survive that."

In other words, he was put through a concentrated dose of what the conspiracy bombards us with every day, and at a certain point enough is enough. Progress be damned, one has to stop and look at how other gay men are actually living and loving, and what marriage can *really* be about, other than love.

Gelfant opens another box, and stops.

"Here's the moment of marital proof," he says of his own now-ended partnership. "This is probably where it all began. I decided we could no longer have stainless steel. We went to an auction. This is early deco twentieth-century silverware. He got the Czech silverware, and I got the Austrian."

I place it in a drawer, and as it slides shut, I wonder how long it will sit there before it gets used again.

"You know what marriage is?" Gelfant asks. "Marriage is accumulating with someone else. With every dish you are more invested. Because it's stuff."

"And of course there's the shared history," I add.

"Forget about the history and all that. It's the stuff that's the problem. You think what about my things, what about the way I live? Marriage was a license to make babies, because procreation was not allowed out of wedlock, and it was a financial arrangement. . . . The modern reality is you can live better. [As a single] you can't live the way you can with two people and the more you do it the more you think this is who you are, it becomes your identity. You can't imagine life any other way. . . . Who wants to move from a five-bedroom house in the Annex [a residential Toronto neighborhood with beautiful tree-lined streets and refurbished hundred-year-old homes] to a one-bedroom loft?"

Gelfant looks around the two-story penthouse that he's only just starting to settle into. "I can't live this way. I won't be able to take holidays. I'm not making that much money. . . . I'd love to have somebody who would pay fifteen hundred a month towards this place, I'd love to have a husband that brings in money, but I have to be in love. To me that's what marriage is. Finding someone with whom you can have a better lifestyle and hopefully you can have great sex."

"Are you willing to give up the great sex?" I ask.

"No! So maybe I'm unmarriable. And I'm not going to do that nonmonogamous thing. . . . And here's the bloody irony. I couldn't do the monogamous thing with the guy I was with. . . . My mother would be angry if she heard me talking. She'd say we were a bunch of self-indulgent [children] and she'd say just grow up, that's not the way life is."

"What does that mean?" I ask.

"You made the decision to be with someone and you make it work," is Gelfant's explanation of his mother's words, adding, "Things may happen but it doesn't matter."

"So is she happy in her marriage?" I press.

Gelfant pauses, and then says with a smirk, "No comment."

A moment later he elaborates. "My sister and I used to ask, which one of us would become like our parents faster, particularly our mother, and the idea was not to win."

And with that I can see that we're going into dangerous territory, because he slides his hand onto my tape recorder and turns it off.

That is where the interview ends, but just like *My Fabulous Gay Wedding*, the story doesn't finish when the tape stops recording. As is often the case, the real story happens off the record. There are several cell phone calls between Gelfant and his ex as each comes across stuff that belongs to the other: baby photos, Czech silverware, a camcorder that they decide they can just throw out.

"That was my partner . . . I mean my ex," he explains, hanging up.

The following day Gelfant calls me to see if he can borrow some screwdrivers. The ex is over, helping him put together the bed they once shared, and the silver bread tray that Gelfant had put in the front hall inset, and jokingly said he'd fill with condoms and lube now that he was single, has been replaced with a series of small framed prints.

I'm not implying the two are getting back together. Gelfant was giddy when telling me about a new crush. But watching them behaving like really good, reliable friends, I am glad to know there is more to love—and less to marriage—than what the conspiracy would have us see, or the hierarchy would have us believe. And while marriage has long been held up as the rite of passage into maturity for straights, I wonder if this transition out of a sexual and romantic relationship into friendship is *the* rite of passage into emotional adulthood for gay men.

Just as gays have turned to straights for models of pair-bonded relationships, perhaps straights should turn to gays for models of civilized breakups, and how to go from even a bad breakup to a good friendship. After all, with so many intersecting circles of friends, lovers, and ex-lovers, gay men often have no choice but to learn how to work through ended romance and into friendship. Instead of celebrating this we tend to put greater value on the concept of love in a boyfriend relationship, rather than the friendship or potential friendship that could follow in the wake of its demise. I hate to even call it a demise. Sometimes it's a perfectly natural transition.

So while we will surely continue to gain greater equality and recognition for gays by playing off the myth that love is a hierarchy, please remember:

We're just pretending.

Husbands and Boyfriends Don't Guarantee Happiness

Fear is the path to the dark side. Fear leads to anger.
Anger leads to hate. Hate leads to suffering.

—Yoda, *The Empire Strikes Back*

ENTER BENOIT.

I met him when I was in my later twenties at an infamous Montreal after-hours club. A huge disco ball twirled overhead, massive speakers shuddered with techno music, and shirtless muscle boys gyrated all around. To see so much physical beauty, close enough to touch, yet still out of reach, was sheer torture. I hunted in their midst for someone to take me in his arms, to take away my gnawing aloneness amid so much seeming togetherness. My E was kicking into high gear.

I started dancing with Benoit, who was much too young for me, so of course he was perfect. Not only did this little twink teach me how to say "I have a hard-on" in French, a lesson never covered by the nuns at the French Catholic elementary school I attended for several years, he fed me a drug more intense than E will ever be.

He made me feel powerful. I had someone holding my hand as we marched through the club. I was no longer searching. I had found, conquered, and been mutually claimed—FOR ALL TO SEE.

Look at me, I've GOT somebody, I wanted to shout.

Others were just there with their friends. I was a step above, and I reveled in it. Just imagine how happy I would be if I could get even higher: boyfriendship.

Or so the conspiracy and the hierarchy of love would have me believe.

By 5 AM I was both exhausted and burning to get naked with him. The language barrier just added to his charm. Everything added to his charm, except perhaps when we finally left and he got his hand stamped at the door—just in case he wanted to get back into the club after we'd finished fucking. I chose to ignore this. Of more immediate concern was the problem posed by his roommate. He really did share a room, a bachelor apartment actually. We tried going to the baths, but got kicked out after about an hour because they were closing, so we tried to keep it quiet on the mattress on the floor next to the pullout couch where his unsuspecting roommate snored.

And then there was Benoit's collection of club pants with specially designed pockets for storing glow sticks. He showed them off proudly.

Tragic reached a whole new level.

Honor thy tricks. I believe this, I really, really do. But would I have been happier if he'd lived alone, in a condo that he owned, and had Prada suits to show off instead of glow stick pants? Had he fit this criteria, would I have gone home to the same friends I'd ditched the night before and raved about this guy as "boyfriend material"? Would I have wanted (or thought I wanted) to see him again and again and again? Yes, yes, and yes.

Rather than having to search out a new guy all the time, I'd have one, a quality one, to love, hold, and show off. He'd help me pick myself up from the bad times and make the good times even better.

At least that's what many of us are hoping for when dreaming of a boyfriend. It's part of the promise of the hierarchy of love, driving us to climb it, making couplehood better than singlehood. But is that the reality? Like many other gay men, I get to hear a *lot* of dissing about relationships from people within relationships. There's the friend who hadn't had sex with his boyfriend in six months, and is now cheating on him. There's the woman in her sixties who's been married for three decades and says "When do I get to start living *my* life?" Yet another woman is thrilled not to be living with an alcoholic anymore.

Forbidden Love

All the same, the belief that a boyfriend or husband is integral to happiness remains a fundamental part of our society. This was vividly verbalized in a 1967 court decision that had everything to do with a different kind of forbidden love. Eight years prior, a heterosexual couple was prosecuted for their interracial marriage, which violated the laws of their home state of Virginia. The newlyweds faced a year in jail unless they agreed to leave the state and not return for twenty-five years. But in '67 the U.S. Supreme Court unanimously ruled Virginia's antimiscegenation law to be unconstitutional. Sixteen states with similar laws were forced to erase them.

As part of the decision, the Court made a declaration that raised the hopes of queer couples wanting to marry, and which underscored an implicit assumption on the state of coupling.

The Court declared, "The freedom to marry has long been recognized as one of the vital personal rights essential to the orderly pursuit of happiness by free men."

Granted, it doesn't say that we *have* to pursue marriage in order to be happy, but it comes real close. And when I have my glow stick moments in gay life, I can't even say that I disagree.

But is getting into a relationship to avoid the Benoits of the world going to make me happy? The sex was fun and it gave me lots to gab about with my best friend the next day. In fact we still refer back to him many years later. Even writing about it now there is a part of me that *enjoys* the story. But I suppose there is a limit.

After all it's not just a conspiracy that drives gays and straights to couple. There are things that suck about being single. There are things that suck about being gay. There are things that suck about being gay *and* single, and which lead to much unhappiness.

Could a relationship be the solution?

The Rating Game

In the case of gay culture, there are many factors that might wear a single guy down.

"All faggots carry in their heads a computer system/ switchboard in which they weigh each other. On the grid we process such factors as height, penis size, ass shape, eyes, clothing, personality, smile, weight, age, skin/hair color, virility, education, intelligence, sun sign, birthplace and so forth. The inexorable computer says: Meet my Fantasy or be gone, what do you think this is, some kind of charity?"

Those words sound like an apt description of a large part of today's gay dating scene, but they were originally published in 1974, long before the stats-driven culture of the World Wide Web, in *Gay Sunshine/Fag Rag* Joint Issue.

It was written by Charles Shively, who adds in the piece, "Since the computer of each faggot is 'fussy' to some degree about who they'll copulate with, the more casual the encounter the less particular they are likely to be. . . . As the stakes go up in the relationship, the standards go up. You might trick with someone in the bushes who has a score of 25, but require a score of 50 before you'd take him home to bed; 65 before you'd fix him breakfast; 69 before you'd actually make it again with him; 75 before you'd live with him; 85 before you'd become his lover; 95 before you'd live with him the rest of your life."

Sounds about right to me. In some respects this boils down to the dreaded "you're too picky" factor that coupled friends poo poo, and which acts as a double-edged sword, putting us below the "standards" of the men we're into, and placing ourselves out of reach of those interested in us. So are gay singles being "too picky"? In some cases, perhaps. Maybe even in many cases. Then again, maybe some gay men have just figured out that with all the compromises involved in a relationship, if they're going to make the necessary sacrifices, the guy had better really knock their socks off, or it just isn't worth it. Or maybe that's just not the kind of relationship that works for them, even if they're trying to get into one.

Still, all this can add up to a nasty cycle that would wear down anyone looking for intimacy.

Dan Renzi, former model and "the gay guy" on MTV's the *Real World Miami* put it to me succinctly in a small and crowded

New York bar in 1997. In the middle of the dance floor were raised podiums with pumped go-go boys gyrating away.

"How am I supposed to get anyone to look at me with these guys around?" I shouted into his ear.

Both his eyes and mine remained locked on the dancers' tan, smooth flesh, our necks craned backward, for they were above us, literally and figuratively. He took a sip from his beer and like a guru on high replied, "It shifts the bell curve."

My testicles shrank inward. In my mind I actually saw a bell-shaped graph, with number of gay men on the x-axis, level of physical perfection on the y-axis. With a click of my inner mouse I watched the whole curve shifting to the right. I probably should've made it a three-dimensional graph with self-esteem on the z-axis, for at that moment mine was crashing. If a successful, witty, and intelligent model/TV star could feel outclassed, what hope was there for the rest of us?

Almost ten years later I glance over at a half-open door in my condo, a washer-dryer combo peeking out. On the inside of the door are six wire shelves, filled with containers of creatine, essential fatty acids, and herbal boosters for human growth hormone and testosterone. It's all natural and available over the counter at health food stores, not that I couldn't get steroids if I wanted to. They've been offered to me twice, but I'm too chicken shit to try them, much as I'd like to. It would be killer on my skin and after spending thousands and thousands of dollars on antibiotics, skin peels, and three courses of treatment on Accutane over a ten-year period, I am not prepared to relive my cystic acne adolescence.

Which is damn frustrating. I've grown into a good-looking guy, but I could be *so* much hotter, tripling the value of my sexual currency out in the marketplace if I had the much coveted plates of dense muscle hinged to my bones that are the VIP pass to the A-list. And for those who think steroids automatically result in big muscle heads who look like they're wearing a gorilla suit, think again. I've been surprised to discover at least one of Toronto's Brad Pitt body doubles was on "the juice." There was also a trick of mine who was quite open about his steroid use, and that of his friends.

Really? I thought as he popped his black market tablet the next morning. *That's all it did for you?*

Don't get me wrong, he looked great, but I was expecting ripped and dense perfection. Which leads me to wonder, after all the circuit parties with artificially pumped bodies, just how warped have my perceptions become? Really warped as it turns out, and even for those who don't take part in this aspect of gay culture (as I never used to and rarely do anymore), there is a ripple effect.

As Dan Renzi put it, all those hot bodies shift the bell curve for *everyone*, even once the party's over, even for those who never went. Steroids raise the bar on hot as well as increasing the number of stupidly hot guys wandering around, and so the overall standard just winds up being that much higher as well.

I used to think that once my own physical transformation took place, *then* I could get into a relationship with an equally hot guy, and *then* I could be happy. Instead I'd often come home from a party alone, depressed, wondering why I *still* wasn't hot enough. But of course this is not about looks and the party scene alone. Coming home from bars, or a cocktail party, or brunch, I wondered if I had failed to "make a connection" with another guy because I wasn't smart enough or funny enough. OK, I also wonder if a tighter T-shirt might've helped.

In writing about the unstated confusion and anxiety of gay sex lives in *Reviving the Tribe: Regenerating Gay Men's Sexuality and Culture in the Ongoing Epidemic,* author Eric Rofes characterizes how the rating game can play out.

"Those who are single increasingly become frustrated with the limited options for meeting appropriate men. Men exchange phone numbers, but never call one another. When one man finds the courage to ask out another who has flirted with him for months, he's surprisingly greeted with sudden disinterest. Trust, honesty, and communication—areas which have never been easy between men—now seem more difficult than ever."

I suspect we all know this rejection cycle a bit too well. Most of us have also been on various sides of this equation. And the cycle Rofes describes remains pretty standard whether one is talking about bar chats, online cruising, or parting glances at the gym. But perhaps where it plays out at its most extreme is at circuit parties, which tend to be full of single (and coupled) hot guys, many of them professionals with the kind of résumés that would leave most single guys thinking: *oh my god, he's perfect! And so is that guy! And that guy!*

Add to that the potential extreme highs and lows of drugs, and the cycle of rejection takes on a whole new intensity, and god knows even a crappy coffee date can leave one feeling incredibly unfulfilled and wondering if a steady partner is the Prozac one should be reaching for.

Chemical Courage

"The drugs just started kicking in," my friend Parker recalls of doing E for the first time last year, at his first circuit party. "And as we were traveling," he says, referring to us snaking our way through a throng of torsos, "We went to the ugly sea," he says, referring to a grouping of guys who were average to below average looking. "I was feeling sensational. And then we went to the beautiful sea, and I said keep traveling. Then I found a spot in the ocean where I was comfortable."

When I initiated Parker into his first circuit experience I had misgivings about introducing anyone to that world, but he was adamant that at thirty-eight years old he was giving it a try, drugs and all. Though it was his wish, I worried that he might wind up exchanging one crutch for another, relationship mania for serotonin delirium. With trepidation I introduced him to Elizabeth (code for E; always use code when talking to your drug dealer on the phone, like, "Yeah, I wanted to party with Elizabeth this weekend, you know, four times. Oh, and I owe her some money. How much do I owe her?" If the cops are listening, I'm sure they must know what's going on, but I guess it offers some protection if it goes to court.)

Which leaves me wondering, when the fuck did I become the guy to hook other people up with drugs, let alone have the expertise to guide them through the more obvious pitfalls of their first trip? I'm the geek who was thrilled when I discovered I could eat my lunch in one of the French language classes at my high school because finally I didn't have to spend that hour eating alone on the front doorstep of some house near my school. And look at the bitch now, a so-called veteran of "the scene," who's had more than one guy pass out in his arms in the middle of making out because of a GHB overdose. There's not even panic in such moments anymore. Get help dragging his ass off the dance floor, get a Coca-Cola from the bar, and try to get some sugar and caffeine into him, maybe put some ice down his underwear, and at the worst call an ambulance and hope he doesn't wind up in a coma.

I knew that ecstasy was not the kind of drug that would put Parker in any such danger, but as he did a hit for the first time I kept a close watch on him, standing a few feet away, letting him bond and dance his ass off with some friends he used to hang out with back when he was still living with his ex of many years whom he now refers to as Lard Ass.

"If you notice that you've stopped sweating, that means your kidneys have shut down, and it's time to take a break and head for the chill out area or you're going to overheat, and that's bad," I'd warned him. "And drink about a bottle of water per hour. More than that and you're *over*loading your kidneys. If you find you never have to pee, that's another sign that they've shut down, and again, time to take a break."

It turns out I'm still a geek, even when I party. As for Parker, his urinary tract was clearly far from his mind as he danced that night away in the arms of a friend of his friends. A huge grin split his face, eyelids drooping over pupils that were slightly glazed. He had the look of one who has gone too far, deep into the land of messiness, or as in his case, an initiate who's simply being carried away by the newness of the sensations coursing through his skin, muscles, and mind.

"You're doing a good thing," a mutual friend assured me as he followed my gaze to Parker and noted the worried expression on my face. I nodded, hoping he was right.

I just hope Parker doesn't wind up liking this too *much.*

"I get it now, I get it!" he shouted on the dance floor, jumping up and down, happier than I've ever seen him. "I'm one of the boys!"

Silencing the Voices of Doubt

"Even though I didn't have sex," Parker tells me days later, "It wasn't about that. It was about jumping over the fence . . . and those voices in my head stopping. The voices of 'you're ugly, you shouldn't be here.' When the voices die, I live for that. When I have this great-looking guy kissing my neck and slam dancing, the voices are gone. They just stopped, and we didn't have sex. I went home alone."

"Is that sense of peace what you got from a relationship?"

"Completely. The voices stop," Parker continues. "You're just tying into something right now. Ten years in that relationship and I didn't have those voices. Now it's up and down. You're hideous, you're this, you're that, and I'm just trying to put it in perspective. By trying to just enjoy your life it redirects the voices, and that's what I'm trying to do, without the dependence of alcohol or E, because I'm not one of those boys, I never was, even when I was eighteen."

His assertion that he's seeking inner peace without the help of recreational drugs sounds like a bit of a contradiction considering the context of his tale, not to mention the residual tingly sensation I get thinking about the fun it can be. But really, two things emerge from our conversation about pursuing happiness within the hurly-burly gay world.

Wanting the voices of doubt to stop.

Feeling like one's life is on hold until they do.

At the extremes, some gay men turn to E (and other drugs over and over again) for these moments of confidence, euphoria, sexual comfort, and sense of self-love, which I don't think anyone would really recommend weekend after weekend, or night after night, for the rest of one's life. Perhaps a boyfriend is a healthier and happier option. But one must be cautious in promoting this, because it creates its own psychological pitfalls. As my friend Steve put it to me between sets at the gym as we discussed this scene: "Cock, coke, and creatine. It's a great way to meet your future ex-boyfriend." Which of course implies that if you stop, *then* you will meet the guy of your dreams, who will then make all your fantasies come true, and then you will be happy, happy, happy. So while the circuit/drug/sex scene is an extreme in gay life, the promise of couplehood as the path to happiness is a repetitive one in all parts of the culture.

But Parker had a long-term relationship that ended long before doing E. Let's see how that panned out for him.

The Trophy Boyfriend

"I was only part of the picture when it was for show for his friends," Parker tells me as he prepares for his students to arrive at his after-school musical theater program. He's explaining to me the dynamics of his last long-term relationship, which lasted a decade and very much took on the form of a marriage before ending four years ago.

"Finally he had that one thing that had eluded him all those years," he says of his ex. "All his friends were in relationships, all his friends lived together, and he was the only single one."

Parker's a classic gay single man. He left a long-term relationship, and would love to get into another, but has come up against a wall of frustration that's left him home alone on many a Friday night, baking cookies from scratch and shoving them into his face as if he were a Hoover.

"What eating disorder?" he quips.

The notes for the song "Mister Cellophane" from the Broadway hit *Chicago* drift into his office from the adjoining studio as his pianist gets his fingers warmed up for this morning's rehearsal. In ones and twos teens start arriving as their parents drop them off from the quintessential suburban minivans. The kids are mostly girls, and four boys, dressed in tights, sweatpants, and T-shirts.

"Set your chairs up for Razzle Dazzle," Parker tells them, waving them along and following them into the studio. On the wall behind him, facing the students, is a cutout from a magazine, featuring the different faces of Cher through the ages. Taped above her is a sign that says FOCUS.

"Amanda, I love your acid stories, but save it for break," Parker says, pointing first to Cher, then to the FOCUS sign, as he does whenever their teen brains start to wander, which is surprisingly infrequently.

The kids laugh, as they do at everything he says. Smiling broadly, Amanda does exactly as she's been told.

"Oh, that's going to Broadway," he says after they rehearse the first number of the morning with the energy of frozen fish. "Better than *Cats*. Do it again."

Parker's one of those guys in his late thirties, talented, funny, energetic, running his own very successful business, connecting with the kids he teaches, working out like a fiend, and he looks better now than when he was in his twenties. But like many single gay men he feels a lack in his life in the areas that a boyfriend really could come in handy: support, intimacy, and affection.

"This is *Chicago* people," he shouts. "Everything's a vaudeville number. Death, the jury, every entrance and exit. Vaudeville! Plié! Smile when you throw that rope that's going to hang her!"

And when a waif of a teen girl with braces and a full set of lungs belts out "I simply cannot do it alone!" Parker's mouth is lip synching along with her, his face dead focused, until the final note falls and we all burst into applause.

He puts his hands together as if in prayer and bows to her.

"See, you just need a little kick in the ass and you're fabulous."

The Show Must Go On

Parker's words to his students are good advice for each and every one of us. Perhaps the love, intimacy, and support many of us crave from a boyfriend are already there, right in front of us, if we open our eyes and shield them from the glare of the gay marriage spotlight that has left us in the shadows. After all, if marriage were a guarantee plug to fill the void, we'd have no need for divorce.

During break I ask him what cover story he wants me to use to explain my presence to his students.

"Just tell them the truth. That you're writing a book." Pause. "About vaudeville."

We laugh.

In this three-ring circus of love, truer words were never spoken.

It's cheat day, so we take a break from our usual pseudo-anorexia and binge eat two-bite brownies. Between mouthfuls he confesses that he's decided to sell the ring from his ex-partner.

"He gave me the ring and it was very important to me, I don't want to knock it, I was so happy when he gave it to me, I showed it to everybody."

He extends his hand toward me, pretending the ring is on his finger, miming the actions of making the band glint in the light. But when he retells the moment his ex presented him with this symbol of unity, there is an underlying dissonance that chafes against his outer cheer.

"He gave me the ring in front of a room of twenty-five people on my birthday. It was a status thing, I would've given it to him alone on a deserted island. But I never gave him a ring, and he always commented on that. But I knew that he was not going to be my husband. I knew I was going to end the relationship.

"The day we broke up I put it in an old jacket pocket which has become my safe. And it's been sitting there ever since. Once a year I look at it, because it reminds me that I was happy at that point, with the status of being in a couple, which I don't have now.

"That is what I'm coming to terms with, the times that I'm lonely now, which is very often, I'm not what I was when I was in that relationship. But there's not one day that I was happy in the relationship. I had good times, but I was very lonely for ten years. I was in it because he was amazing for me on paper. He was exactly all that I'd ever wanted, and it was for show, and I knew exactly what I was doing. It was my own fault for staying."

But in the end, the relationship was not consistent, and there wasn't the intimacy, connection, and support for which he'd hoped. And in a way, there was also another man in his partner's life.

"He has a very good buddy, platonic, no sexual interest." It later emerges that Parker's ex did in fact at one point have a thing for this friend, but it was not reciprocated. "He would use him as his confidant and best friend. Many times he would leave me and travel with him, and not with me, but travel with me when he wanted to, with other couples, to make it look like we were happy. He didn't understand why I was upset with him, but I let him go many times. His birthday was coming up and he wanted to go to France with his friend and not me. And I gave him an ultimatum. I was tired of telling people, our friends, why I was stuck at home again. I wasn't jealous of their relationship, the guy hated me, and trashed me, and before he left—you're going to laugh—I was just starting to learn the Internet, he had an account, I had one, I logged on, and boom, there was an email from the friend. I did not go searching for it, I did not go snooping for it, but here was this email, this whole correspondence, back and forth.

"Every bit of information which I had confided to my boyfriend, which I thought was a natural trust, about my financial life—revealed; my sexual positions and favors and personal life was told to this person who hated me and who used everything as ammunition against me. His friend went on and on and on about how he could do better, much better than me, I read this in a four-page letter. The computer was completely covered in tears, I couldn't believe that, ten years of trust and of . . ."

Even four years after the fact tears start building in his eyes and his voice catches ever so slightly.

"What I thought the relationship was, was gone in this e-mail. I didn't want to tell him that I read it. I closed my mouth. I told him you have a choice. You go to Europe on your birthday, and you come home and there's not me. And he said I'm going to Europe. And I said OK. He didn't think I would leave, like all the other trips, when I'd come home and there'd be a note just out of the blue: *I didn't want to tell you because you'll be mad, but I'm in Paris right now.*"

But this time, when he came home from Paris, Parker was gone.

"He couldn't believe it," Parker tells me, "because the little puppet grew up."

Not Waiting for Happiness

Break time is over, and Parker's out playing Mother Goose with his gaggle of goslings, their teenage quacks and clucks echoing as he steers them out of the front lobby and back to the studio.

"You're going to be atrocious," he warns them of the next scene. "But that's OK. We're going to fix that."

I follow behind, musing on how he's changed since I first met him a few years ago at the gym. He was chewing out his trainer as he prepared to loan her his Abbacadabra CDs.

"These are imports. Don't you *dare* lose them!"

Years later, as he wraps up rehearsals for the day and the teens file out, we overhear one of the girls say, "I think I'm a fag hag."

She's fourteen. Even the girls who like boys who like boys are starting younger these days.

We laugh and he says to me, "Aren't they an amazing bunch of kids?"

The pride shines in his eyes, and he can't stop bragging about how talented they are. And it's true. Even in half-a-day, through the process of repetition, I've watched them improving, witnessed them *getting* it. It's going to be an amazing show, high kicks and all.

The rehearsals are a bitch, but Parker makes them fun, and it's clear his kids love him as much as he does them. They're not waiting for curtain call to have a good time. Nor is Parker—not anymore.

"It's time to go shopping," he announces, reminding me of the ring his ex-boyfriend gave him.

Cashing it in is his symbolic farewell.

"I will sell the ring and buy a really fabulous pair of running shoes, which I do not need."

At first we try a discount footwear outlet, and he turns into one long monologue as we wander through aisles of shoe boxes stacked shoulder high.

"For the last four years I have wanted to pick up my life where it left off—being in a relationship, I mean—going for dinner parties, being very social, having someone, feeling important, but with a different person. That didn't happen, not even an inkling of anything. Everything has failed, at least that's how I felt, and I've just realized that for the last four years, wonderful things have happened to me, but I've always been convinced that nothing wonderful has happened to me and the last four years have been absolutely horrible."

And then in an about-face Parker declares, "I'm sorry. I just can't deal with this." He throws a pair of Diesel-inspired knockoffs back into a box.

"We're going to Yorkville," he announces, referring to Toronto's chichi shopping district, where FCUK meets Hugo Boss.

"I'm more open to the world, I'm in the moment more often, and I'm enjoying being in that particular moment with that particular person, as opposed to having an agenda," he tells me. "It's so tiresome, as you know, always having an agenda, and other gay men have it, but that doesn't mean that I have to have it, and when you lose the agenda, you realize it is working, even if I don't pick up. In my old thinking I would've called that a failure."

But now he is met with success, waltzing into a shoe store more to his liking, and instantly gravitating toward a pair of white Pumas with tasteful green accents.

He cradles the sneaker like a new lover, still talking but not looking at me, balancing the Pumas this way and that.

He tries on the shoes, modeling them for me by twisting his foot this way and that. "I hope I run into my ex during Pride while I'm wearing these."

Some might take this a sign that he still defines himself to a considerable degree by what his ex thinks of him, but ten years is too long for a simple pair of shoes to simply erase. To be honest, though, even as he talks about the ex, he's far more focused on the new purchase than on the imagined encounter.

"I want to add that I'm not on Prozac," Parker says, reaching for his wallet. "I'm not on drugs. And I really recommend that gay men who have this crisis, and it is a crisis—you're successful, you're handsome and funny and witty and intelligent, and yet you feel incomplete and it can be really depressing. It's not funny when you're at home chowing down on cheesecake, it's depressing. . . . I recommend, just really start enjoying your life."

It's good advice that he's learning to follow.

He was single when we met, and I've never known him in a relationship, but I have watched him struggle to negotiate the challenges of a single gay man who's back in the emotional garberator of the dating scene. He's cute and has a nuclear-powered reactor that just doesn't quit in the sack, but he'll be the first to admit he's not an Abercrombie model, and often winds up feeling like the proverbial Mr. Cellophane when out at the bars. Which brings us full circle, to "the scene," and the wearing affect it can have on gays, single and coupled alike.

At the same time, as he so clearly demonstrates, domesticity can break a man down, too, it just happens in greater privacy, Desperate Homo Housewife style. But we are still dreadfully silent about this.

When it is discussed, the general consensus among the gay men I've spoken with is that a good relationship is better than no relationship, but no relationship is *way* better than a bad one.

But I can't help but wonder if this would be the attitude if the hierarchy of love did not exist and the promise of happiness it offers were examined more critically. Could it be that the *promise* of coupled happiness is leading to misery as singles wait to be happy?

The Boyfriend Within

"People put their life on hold waiting for someone to give them permission to have a good experience," Brad Gooch tells me from his home in New York. Gooch is the infamous author of the wildly successful book *Finding the Boyfriend Within,* so it's not surprising that our conversation ranges from dating to one-night stands to emotional bankruptcy.

Like many people, I picked up *Finding the Boyfriend Within* because I figured it would lead to a boyfriend without. Gay friends and acquaintances disparaged me when they saw me with a copy. Then on the sly they would ask if it was any good and could they borrow it.

I'm not saying it changed my life, but nor did it radically transform the life of the author himself. In Gooch's own words, "It isn't so much that my circumstances have changed . . . just that my attitude toward the usual stuff has been transmogrified in a completely positive way. Life with the Boyfriend Within hasn't become unrecognizably different, just smoother, warmer, and more focused and clear."

It is in part what many of us are looking for from that special someone we hope will complete our lives. In a sense *Finding the Boyfriend Within* is a starter manual for those looking to learn how to love as a single gay man, *not* as a single gay man pining for a relationship.

"What we often mean when we say, 'I'm looking for a boyfriend' is that we're looking for that warm feeling of happiness, or contentment, or peace and inner satisfaction, for that turning of the heart into a pond of golden nectar," writes Gooch.

Gooch's words paint in stark relief the system of rewards and punishments I'd set up for myself. If I got through school, got that degree, got a good job, worked on my social skills, got in shape, and reduced my impact on the environment by recycling and composting, then for sure I'd meet my soul mate. The boyfriend was both the accomplishment and the reward wrapped in one. The two would come together.

All or nothing.

So I was stuck with nothing.

It's a pretty dire and soulless way to live.

I remember one night being tired of it. Tired of putting my life on hold as I tried to fit a specific image of what it meant to be in love. I was full of romantic notions and was determined to wait for "the one" before going all the way. Blow jobs were fine, but no penetration in the derriere. That was special. But after six years of pining I couldn't keep putting my life on a dusty shelf and I did what any self-respecting gay man would do.

I went to the Barn, a bar in Toronto known for its surly staff and fast pickups. I met a cute guy, he took me into the light to make sure I was up to snuff, then I brought him home, told him to fuck me, and endured it by imagining I was in an aerobics class and the instructor was shouting *three more, two more, one more!* with every thrust. I later kissed my trick goodbye and crossed "take it up the ass" off my to-do list.

Gay sex has often been called a political act. If so, this was not a *gay* political act, but a gay *single's* political act. It was a painfully empowering moment, one that allowed me to expand what my body would later come to enjoy in terms of erotic play, without waiting another moment to get started.

Still, it would've been nice if he'd called the next day, or stayed over so I could wake up on Saturday morning with my head on his chest.

So, would I have been *happier* if it had been a boyfriend that had initiated me into receiving anal sex? Would the experience have been *better*? Maybe. Maybe not. It could've been worse for all I know. All I can really say is this is how my life has unfolded. No judgments. No comparing to what did not happen. This is my story. And as the next chapter relates, that kind of attitude might be the true key to life-satisfaction for the single gay man.

5. The Happiest Gay Singles Are "Single by Choice"

We have this prejudice that if someone's single and wants to be single they're seen as being cold.

—Andrew Holleran, *fab*,
Valentine's issue, 2004

IT'S THE END OF a day of churning out news copy at CBC Newsworld, Canada's answer to CNN. I come home to an empty apartment where I am greeted by no messages on my answering machine. Deena, the woman who apparently had this phone number before I did, gets more calls than I do. I mix a protein shake because I can't be bothered to cook dinner for just myself—there's not even anything good on TV to keep me company, and a DVD is too much commitment. The sound of a passing siren wails from outside and I begin to wonder, is *this* the story of my life?

Stories are powerful things when it comes to happiness, as psychologist Andrew Hostetler well knows. Hostetler specializes in the role of self-determination in life, constraints on individual choice, as well as gender and sexual development in adulthood. All three come into play in his 2001 study, "Single Gay Men: Cultural Models of Adult Development, Psychological Well-Being, and the Meaning of Being 'Single by Choice'."

As he points out in his illuminating research, even though singles comprise up to 60 percent of the gay population, research has essentially focused on partnership, and "academic silence on gay male singlehood has been deafening. . . . On the rare occasions when gay singles appear in the literature, it is usually in the context of a comparison with their coupled counterparts, measured against whom they typically appear deficient."

To illustrate this point he quotes from the movie/play *Jeffrey*.

"You're gay. You're single. It isn't pretty."

This attitude is in part what inspired Hostetler to take on the topic of gay singlehood. While the self-help books examine why relationships end, and how to keep them going, he looks at why some gay guys aren't actively trying to get into them in the first place. He believes that these gay men, the ones who feel they are single by choice, will be the happiest among the noncoupled cohort, and the best adjusted. This "choice," he asserts, is a form of "narrative solution."

So Who Are These "Voluntarily" Single Gay Men?

As I look at the army of gay singles, I wonder: who's hoping to escape the land of singletons to join the couples camp across the border? Who's making it over bar-life barbed wire and past first-date land mines? Who's getting blown up and shredded by emotional shrapnel? And who's happiest staying put?

Sociologist Peter J. Stein puts it more scientifically, breaking singlehood into the categories of voluntary temporary, voluntary stable, involuntary temporary, and involuntary stable.

As someone who's never had a boyfriend, I can confidently say I fall into the "stable" category of singlehood. In fact when I tell people the title of this book, and they say "so what happens if you get into a relationship?" I just have to laugh. "After more than three decades of not having a boyfriend, I'm not worried," I reassure them. There's an odd catharsis that follows this statement, because suddenly, to my own surprise, I find myself really not worried. It reminds me that I've been doing this singles thing for so long, I'm good at it. I *like* it. This is my steady state. To get into a relationship, now that would be weird.

Maybe Hostetler's on to something. His thesis is that those who identify as "single by choice," whether they consider that choice to be permanent or for the time being, will be happier than those who perceive themselves as involuntarily single, either for the short or long haul. In other words, those who stepped off the treadmill will be in a better mental place than those who feel they were thrown off, or never allowed on in the first place.

He also points out that these categories are not static, and that singles can move from one to the other as circumstances change with time.

As for his grand conclusion to this hypothesis, well, he says the answer is "elusive," and that to be single by choice is a "complex and multifaceted experience." He also points out that within a larger society that pressures people into coupling as part of the "normal" life course, he is suspicious of anyone who says they have "chosen" to be single. He wonders if the concept of choice is a form of rationalization or a "self-deception."

"I suspected that individuals might claim to be single by choice as a means of ego-defense and irrespective of how satisfied they are with their lives as single people . . . remaining single beyond a certain age represents a social problem that requires an explanation."

Hostetler takes it further.

"Behind a politely phrased inquiry as to whether or not one is voluntarily single lurks the unspoken sentiment, 'How could anyone *choose* to be single?'" He also points out that there is a large amount of pressure to justify this state and answer this question with a sense of integrity. "In other words, we would expect there to be a fair amount of social and psychological pressure on the 'partnerless' to say they choose, and/or are content with, their single lives."*

Just as he suspected, many respondents wound up contradicting themselves with regards to the "choice" to be single. Sixty percent said it was their choice to be single, and yet 83 percent of respondents said they would like to have a relationship, and just over 60 percent of respondents said they were currently looking for a relationship. An almost equal number said they would be happier in a couple.

Thus to cut through the confusion that can be brought on by such an ego-driven question, he assesses *true* voluntary singlehood using the "Integration of Single Status Measure," which he describes as the singlehood equivalent of methods used to gauge marital satisfaction. Out of the hundred men surveyed, he found nineteen whom he considers "truly" voluntarily single.

"Not only are they happy and satisfied with their lives as single gay men, not only are they not actively searching for

*About 70 percent of the almost 100 men surveyed were white, 17 percent African American, almost 10 percent Latino, and just over 4 percent were Asian, all drawn from the Chicago area. Most were middle class and highly educated, ranging in age from 35 to 82 years old. Seventeen percent reported being HIV positive, and most of these had been diagnosed with AIDS.

partnership, but some of these men even claim they *prefer* being single." He isolated several characteristics that these men shared in common. He found they had considerable social and financial resources, along with a perception that a future relationship was not likely.

Hostetler goes on to ask if these are accurate factors by which to measure happiness and psychological well-being.

"Given the inherent difficulty of embracing a non-normative social status, there is surely a developmental process at work here, particularly given the importance of past experiences and future expectations. Above and beyond the statistical relationships between variables, what is the interpretive process by which someone convinces himself that social and developmental norms regarding intimate relationships do not apply to him?"

The Narrative Solution

With further analysis Hostetler, found that income and social support were *not* the most important factors in determining whether a single gay man was happy and psychologically well-adjusted to his status. Instead he refers to "narrative solutions" that emerged during his research, a reworking of life history if you will.

In other words, the happily single gay men were looking back at the events in their lives as if they were the starring role in a modern-day film, following the twists and turns of their own plotline to create a self-understanding of how they'd wound up where they were. Once they'd broken it down into sequential, or even nonsequential steps, it seemed logical that they'd landed in a state of singleness, for in retrospect, that was the path they took, either by choice or by circumstances beyond their control.

"Beneath the apparent interpretive chaos, a coherent storyline emerges, dramatizing a primary tension in . . . life between 'narrow escapes' and deliberate decisions." He says the end result of this back and forth "narrative tug-of-war" is a form of "ego-integrity" and sense of well-being. The ego is OK and not dumping on itself because the individual has managed to transition into the feeling that it makes sense that he's single, rather than telling himself the story that he's come up short.

I witnessed this over the course of my own interviews while researching this book, including in conversation with David Gale, who hosted *Second Time Around*, a dating show about straight people who were looking to get back into a relationship.

"I thought it was very ironic that they had this perpetually single gay guy hosting this show about straight dating, but I could certainly dole out the wisdom," Gale tells me.

David Gale's other credits include hosting the cooking show *Loving Spoonfuls*, where he'd go to the home of a different ethnic grandmother each week and prepare some sort of dish from their native culture.

"We'd dance and we'd sing and I'd flirt with them," said Gale.

But his true claim to fame was dancing in the original commercial for Diet Pepsi when aspartame was first introduced.

"It changed the nature of diet drinks forever."

Now many years later, it's not just the world of calorie-reduced carbonation that will never be the same again. As he goes through his love history with me, I see the interesting back-and-forth debate that goes on in so many of us, second-guessing himself at times, asking questions as much as providing statements, just like every episode of *Sex and the City*, for that is the process that leads to a sense of resolution.

As Hostetler noticed, his subjects almost seemed to be selling their stories, as much to him as to themselves.

In one moment Gale's telling me, "My standard line is: I'm very picky. The reality is I have a full and rich and active life. I'm not lonely, I'm not at want for something to do or for friends or for love. I have lots of love in my life, close, close friends that are my family here. One of my best friends is my roommate, we have a situation where we'll go to the movies, have dinner together, and it's a cohabitating arrangement."

All of which sounds great. But then it flips. "It's certainly slowed down the drive to find a partner, which is not a good thing."

On the other hand, he points out that he's all too often on the receiving end of having to hear about other people's relationship problems, which undermines the attractiveness of the day-to-day reality of such a coexistence.

"I think, god, I don't want to deal with that. Which is of course just an excuse," he adds seconds later. "You have to step up to the plate at some point."

"Are you going to?" I asked.

"Tomorrow," he replied, totally deadpan, barely needing an ounce of his improv training for his immediate and facetious comeback.

But only moments later . . .

"I have to backtrack," he confessed. "There have been times when I reflect on my life as it is and what I have and what I might be missing, and I think I'm a lucky guy with a job that's worth doing and enviable and I'm successful at it, and I have a home and a son and great friends and right now I'm in a situation where I have a roommate so I have companionship, so what am I missing really? And I'm missing perhaps the Hollywood version of romance and I think I'd like to go to a romantic dinner with my partner or travel and walk along the Seine with my lover or just walking along the beach, doing those things that all look like some kind of postcard. But is that the reality? I mean it certainly can happen and it would be nice to experience that and sometimes I have fears. I don't want to be a lonely old guy. But then again my parents are together still and this year will be their fiftieth anniversary and they separate for five months a year. He likes the warm weather and goes to Palm Springs for five months. She goes for two weeks. She's got her volunteering and her grandchildren and she likes her life in Winnipeg."

At first it feels like he's jumping back then springing forward with his thoughts and opinions, but it becomes clear that he is circling, spiraling in fact, closer to his own truth with each revolution.

"I think that people are more comfortable in a coupled situation. It's the way people in this society function, so when people are not in a pair-bonding relationship they don't know how to deal with it. Maybe some people are just single people, and maybe I'm just a single person, and maybe that's the way I function, and maybe I'm too heavily influenced by the outside world which says you're not complete until you're in a relationship, you're not experiencing life until you're married. Who's to say that I don't have it right?"

One participant in Hostetler's research encapsulates the notion of this type of narrative solution with the words "I've *come* to the realization that I'm single because that's what I *wanted* (my emphasis)." This shift in perception is everything. There is a long line of research that shows that people are often happy with what they have, until they start comparing themselves to other people, and the unhappiness arises when they start focusing on what they *don't* have. Thus Hostetler's narrative solution fits what is in essence a narrative problem. "The personal narrative or life history becomes the primary means through which the individual attempts to strike a balance between cultural expectations, personal goals and desires and experience-as-lived."

"I mourned the life that I thought I was going to have," David Gale explains to me of when he fully came out of the gay closet in his thirties. Until then he'd still been seeing women but found he was more emotionally connected with men. "I thought, well, I guess I'm not going to have kids and be the dad I always assumed I would be. As much as I loved children and wanted to do that . . . I didn't want to get married to someone I didn't love and bring children into the world and have to deal with all that, and I really didn't want to be a single parent, so I really mourned that idea. People weren't really having children in gay relationships at that time. Some lesbians had started, but they were quiet, and gay men weren't. They were dying a lot."

And yet the man whose dance moves helped revolutionize low-carb sodas has been a father for almost three years now, coparenting with a lesbian couple who take care of their son, Eli, except for once a week, when he comes to spend time with his dad.

Hostetler points out the "aesthetic" difference between *giving up* and *giving in*, which I see echoed in Gale's story.

"Stuff happens." Gale shrugged when I pointed out that in many ways, in his beautifully done home in a residential Toronto neighborhood well outside the city's gay borough, he's very much living the life he's told me he dreamed of. "I'm living like a divorced heterosexual," he said, adding with a smirk, "Maybe the person I needed to be is a divorced straight man."

Seven Cock-Tales

David Gale's narrative is a good example of how one can strike a balance between life as one expected it to be and life as one is actually living it.

In terms of what other stories (good and bad) gay men are telling themselves, it does vary among individuals, but in the final analysis, only seven different tales emerged in Hostetler's research study. Hostetler admits that his sample size for life histories was small, twenty men, but he also points out that other research indicates "life-stories become somewhat repetitive in content relatively quickly."

With that in mind, he highlights the following recurring motifs. He emphasizes the narratives that follow are not mutually exclusive and one or more often work hand in hand with others.

The Personal Past: This appeared in eleven out of twenty of the life history narratives the study looked at. An unhappy childhood, a "delayed adolescence," an overbearing mother or parents who divorced would all be explanations for one's current singleness that would fit into this category. In other words, something like Daddy didn't love me enough, so now I can't love enough to be with another man, or I didn't have enough experimental fun while in the closet so I'm playing catch-up.

The Collective Past: This appeared in five out of twenty life histories, and puts the individual's plotline within the context of the sociohistorical events taking place around him. For example, I sometimes feel that my ability to be intimate was shattered by the AIDS epidemic because it created a fear in me of gay sex long before I ever came out. Psychoanalyst Richard Isay goes so far as to point to a developmental lag in some gay men because of fear of AIDS. Other examples include those who came out when there were no role models for gay relationships. Most of the men in this category were over sixty.

Learning from Experience: This theme manifested in seven of the twenty stories. These individuals have had at least one serious relationship and don't want to repeat mistakes of the past and don't want to be in a relationship simply for the sake of being with someone. "The 'learning from experience theme,'" says Hostetler, "is the 'personal past' theme turned inside out, a developmental narrative in which the individual takes responsibility for and control over his life."

Particular Sexual Tastes: This story appeared in seven out of twenty of the plotlines. "These tastes may be somewhat exotic, and therefore reduce the pool of potential partners, or they may simply be difficult— or even impossible—to realize in the context of a long-term relationship." This includes attractions to specific races, body types, ages, as well as fetishes. I've no doubt I can get that nineteen-year-old body-builder, and yes, we *will* be very happy together. Or as a friend who's into online wrestling hookups told me, lots of guys into that scene say they haven't found someone who can satisfy their emotional needs *and* lock their heads in a decent scissors hold.

Still Searching: Eight out of twenty men fit into this category. Some of them expressed surprise at still being single, some considered themselves on hiatus, or just taking a break from dating.

Loners: This theme appeared in nine of twenty cases. "These are men who believe that their single status at least partially reflects a long-standing dispositional or temperamental characteristic, which they trace throughout their adult lives if not back to childhood."

Aloners: This is a term he used for men who he believes have *become* socially isolated with time and age, as opposed to disposition, and often look back to a more glorious and social time in their lives. This theme also appeared in nine out of twenty histories.

In other words, out of twenty men, eighteen were either loners or aloners, in addition to falling into other categories

listed above. Hostetler is leery of drawing psychological con-
clusions from this data, as he points to studies that indicate
that singles are not "selected out" from partnership because of
a "personality pattern."

It's all very interesting, but as I sit on my couch, alone with
my protein shake, I wonder how much of this I really believe.
Can a simple story really be the key to a person's happiness,
namely my own?

In speaking with Andrew Hostetler about his study five
years after it was published, I learn that he's had a bit more
time to digest his own research. He tells me the gay singles
who truly seemed the happiest among his research participants
were those who were a bit younger and who felt that they were
temporarily off the market. He also emphasized that none of
the participants came to him with a pro-singles agenda. None
of them expressed at any point that they felt that singlehood
was their destiny when they came out. "There was not a single
person who told the story that they set out to be single. No
one was very politically minded." There were no "Queer
Nation or ACT UP leftovers" with heteronormative angst,
though Hostetler would've been interested in talking with
someone with that background.

In fact at least one research participant quite openly was
hoping to use Hostetler as a matchmaking service. "He wasn't
interested in hearing about the results. He was interested in
getting hooked up with other guys in the study."

And in envisioning a possible life for himself as a single gay man (Hostetler is now in a relationship), "there wasn't anyone who I would aspire to be like in ten or twenty years," he says of the guys in his study, repeating a complaint a friend made to him once.

"There are no single role models."

The complaint is an interesting one, especially as many used to say there were no gay couple role models.

But Hostetler does point to a bias in the research participants. He did his best to get a random sample, but he found that several of the men who took part were seeking some sort of therapeutic value from the research. They almost seemed to be trying to figure out their singlehood while sharing their life history with Hostetler.

When he mentions this, I realize my own incredibly unscientific research sample has been even more biased, but in the opposite direction. I have intentionally sought out gay men who seem content in their singlehood and who I *would* look to as role models, because I wanted to know how they were successfully negotiating this often rocky terrain. And Hostetler's friend is right: we do need single role models, if only to know that it's possible to be gay and single and happy and dignified. To know that we are not destined to be lonely old queens, which is the story the conspiracy would still have us believe.

A narrative solution, for a narrative problem.

Wanting to Be with Someone Is Natural—Not Wanting to Stay with Him Is, Too

Nothing is easier than to admit in words the truth of the universal struggle for life, or more difficult. . . . Yet unless it be thoroughly engrained in the mind, I am convinced that the whole economy of nature, with every fact on distribution, rarity, abundance, extinction, and variation, will be dimly seen or quite misunderstood.

—Charles Darwin, *On Natural Selection*

WHEN I WAS SEVEN years old my family had an informal ritual on Saturday and Sunday mornings. My older brother and younger brother, both close in age to myself, would crawl into bed with my parents. I tried taking part, but there were limbs everywhere, heavy nose breathing, and with five bodies in one bed I instantly overheated.

I retreated to my own bed and left them to their puzzling gathering, within which I found neither comfort nor merit.

An exercise that I found more to my liking was at night. After my mother would tuck me in, sometimes she'd lie down next to me for a bit. There was a feeling of safety and security in such moments. But there was also a fine line that was far too easily crossed.

Sometimes she'd fall asleep before I did.

At that point I'd be stuck listening to her snore, my body squished between her and the wall, our combined body heat making me feel like I was choking.

So one night, as she lay next to me, I heard her breathing starting to slow, which was a sure sign that she was about to fall asleep. With my pudgy little hand I gave her a nudge on the shoulder. When she came to I primly informed her, "You can go now."

It is an apt example of a time when close became *too* close, and a deft ear for heavy breathing was the difference between a good night's rest and being trapped while someone else snored.

And so I wonder, could my current singleness date back to a time when I'd secretly pick my nose and wipe it onto the cartoon lions and tigers on my bedroom wallpaper? Or could my singleness go further back, to the womb? Could there be a biology of singleness? Maybe this is my natural state of being, or at the very least my predisposition. And yet I used to fantasize about having a boyfriend to the point where it was torture. Then again, I also used to have heterosexual fantasies about muscle guys with women—it's just that my focus was always on the guy.

Just as the time came for me to leave my heterosexual fantasies behind in order to embrace my inner homo nature, perhaps the time has now come to leave my coupled imaginings in the past and embrace my inner singles nature.

Love Is a Story and Love Is a Chemical

I used to picture walking hand in hand with a guy down the street. I'd jump cut from that to him coming to my family's Christmas dinner.

At his parents' place, I'd envision myself peeling carrots with his mom (something I'd only do under protest with my own mother) and I'd play the hero by smoothing over the usual tension amongst the in-laws with a witty bon mot. His father, an archetypal patriarch, hated me of course, though even he would come to value my pearls of wisdom over the years, even if I didn't like drinking beer or going hunting.

And then there would be the fights between myself and my man. Yes, I imagined those, too. Sometimes he would cheat on me. Other times, I'd cheat on him. It would either end with bitter tears and moving boxes, or bitter tears, hot sex, and an engagement ring. Tragically, there was a car accident not long after the wedding/breakup. I visited him in the hospital even though all his relatives turned on me, demanding to know where I got the nerve to shed tears when I was the one who'd ruined his life with my deviant ways. Naturally there was a hunky male nurse in a tight white uniform who saw it all and found a place in his heart for my stoic dignity. I on the other hand didn't even notice him, as all my energies were focused on my husband/ex. He was badly burned and ultimately succumbed to his wounds, leaving me with only my memories of us antiquing together, buying a now useless set of crystal champagne glasses for two. My eulogy was very moving (his lesbian aunt insisted I be there, and nobody crosses that dyke) and even his father started to cry at my words.

Years later I'd run into the hunky nurse, and start it all over again.

It's all very Romeo and Juliet in its own way. I blame the Moors. They're the ones who brought romanticism into Western culture when they occupied Spain, and I damn the French troubadours for spreading romanticism in the twelfth and thirteenth centuries. I add a curse on gay men for being the perfect suckers for the romantic dream of love, which emphasizes total individual freedom in selecting a lover, often with an overtone of some "mysterious destiny" and complete social disregard.

I mean what could be gayer than to believe in individual freedom to select a partner, and then to disregard mainstream social conventions in that pursuit? Is that not the very choice we make by coming out of the closet? No wonder Andrew Holleran described us in *Dancer from the Dance* as "a community whose citizens are more romantic, perhaps, than any other on earth." In fact, while some argue that to come out is an explicit expression of one's sexual desire for the same sex, I'd counter there is also a strong draw toward consummating romantic ideals that we are told to have for women but which we instead have for men.

Building this fantasy of a future life, with a perfect mate, certainly sustained me in the closet.

My third and most useful therapist, a social worker who specialized in working with gay men, put it to me this way when I asked for some feedback: "I get the sense that you're angry, and that you feel like you're *entitled* to something."

It was the verbal slap in the face I needed to snap me out of the haze clouding my brain and deceiving me into believing that a boyfriend was my due. I suddenly realized I was *not* entitled to anything. Not a god damn thing. But believing that I was, and not getting what I was entitled to, left me furious and feeling both cheated and somehow lied to. It also blinded me (and sometimes still blinds me) to the reality of romance.

Romance is a story that we build and a fantasy that we live. It's also chemically driven.

It helps to remind myself that my feelings of elation from a crush or a charged flirtation come from the release of a natural amphetamine (i.e., speed) called phenylethylamine (PEA).

"When you're in love, you actually are drugged without realizing it!" writes Joe Kort, who specializes in the psychotherapy of gay men, and is the author of *10 Smart Things*

Gay Men Can Do to Improve Their Lives. In fact, one study that used brain scans found that the part of the brain activated by "love" was the same part activated by snorting coke.

But each time PEA is released it's less powerful, and lasts for a shorter period of time. When the drug wears off, the honeymoon's over.

"Romantic love is supposed to end—for everyone," he writes. Many just give up when the high dissipates and it turns out they don't actually like the other person all that much when the masks are dropped, and they realize a longer relationship requires a deeper connection and a lot of hard work. But things can be protracted when couples break up and get back together again, sometimes repeatedly, their reunion triggering fresh doses of PEA. In more extreme cases, where a craving for PEA needs to be satisfied to be engaged with life, some doctors might actually refer to them as "love junkies," a syndrome that can be fueled by a chemical imbalance in the brain.

My interpretation of this? Wanting to be with someone is natural. Not wanting to stay with him is, too.

This doesn't mean I've become a total bitter Sheila. I'm actually *less* bitter now, because the ending of romance, or a date that sputters into nothing, feels more like part of a natural cycle as opposed to some sort of failure or defect on my part.

When I meet a guy I'm into I still get excited, and I still have my little melodramatic fantasies, but the old storyline of boy meets boy meets redneck parents meets tragic car accident fatality meets porn star nurse has become a bit faded. In addition to this grainy film playing on a loop, I take a moment to picture something beyond romance, like waking up to someone *every* morning, and going to bed with that same someone *every* night. Perhaps flashing back to when my whole family (except me) would cuddle in bed, I start to shudder at the mere thought of such constant proximity, and when I lie in the middle of my queen-size mattress alone, I pause to appreciate the quiet stillness, disturbed only by my chronic overnight flatulence. Again, I am thankful to be alone. At Christmas I remember to thank Jesus that I have only one family to visit, buy presents for, and receive presents from, as we will all likely have to take back at least some of what we were given, to be exchanged for things we actually want.

And on those occasions when I am lonely, or sad, or horny, I remind myself that there are people with boyfriends who are also lonely, sad, and horny. Trust me. I meet them on Manhunt.com.

But as Andrew Hostetler tells me in conversation about his own experience as a single gay man, it's easy to understand this all on an intellectual level. It's tougher to get it emotionally. And now that he is in a relationship it "shifts the spectrum. My baseline's a little bit happier."

Obviously there is something beyond the rush of romantic tales and PEA, something that is longer lasting.

It's called oxytocin.

The Cuddle Chemical

I am *obsessed* with oxytocin. Well, I'm obsessed with the *concept* of oxytocin.

In her book *A Natural History of Love* Diane Ackerman talks about this "cuddle chemical," so-called because of the pleasure it gives from cuddling and during sex. I believe that oxytocin, far more so than PEA, puts love into context. While romantic love (as embodied by PEA) is revered, it is also disparaged if it "fails" to develop further. When we speak of "developing further" what we generally mean is something a little less Romeo and Juliet, that involves a bit more real life support through challenging times, as well as a deep-seated affection and hopefully some respect for the other person. We often speak of such a relationship in very practical terms, such as what it brings into one's life in the form of support and companionship. At times, though, there can also be a tone, implicit or explicit, that because this kind of relationship takes effort, that those who are in one are *workers*, that perhaps they have some sort of work *ethic* that singles may be lacking.

Oxytocin puts a different spin on things. Oxytocin is the payoff in the form of feeling good. And some people are almost certainly getting paid more than others. Biology, after all, has never belonged to a union.

For one thing, oxytocin has a larger effect on women, but even in men it can quintuple during orgasm. It also plays a role in women during and after childbirth, helping to form attachments between mother and baby. Researchers have also found that the number of oxytocin receptors in some species plays a role in how attached they become to those they mate with.

For example, prairie voles are an exception among mice, living in couples, staring into each other's eyes, and rearing their young together.

Turns out the monogamous prairie vole has way more oxytocin receptors than most other mice species. And "unlike other hormones, oxytocin can be generated both by physical and emotional cues—a certain look, voice, or gesture is enough—and can become conditioned to one's personal love history. The lover's smell or touch may trigger the production of oxytocin," says Ackerman.

She goes so far as to ask if loners might have lower oxytocin levels. It's also possible that some people have fewer oxytocin receptors. Whatever the case, I am quite convinced that some people chemically get more out of a relationship than others, which is totally fine—all the power to them—but why would I make the necessary sacrifices for that kind of job if I'm only getting half the pay, especially when there's other emotional employment out there promising me a much more suitable salary for my biological disposition?

As a self-declared loner, I wonder if some of us simply get our comforting opiates from the Zen of solitude, free from the bustle of mindless chatter and the demands partners often place on each other, robbing one of the possibility of immersing oneself in the pleasure of one's own company.

Certainly in Andrew Hostetler's research on single gay men

nine out of twenty of the men who took part in his life history section considered themselves loners, and felt this predisposition had contributed to their singleness.

Whether this is inherited or learned, I'm not sure. After all, as one single-for-life gay man pointed out, "We get good at what we do. To be alone and happy is a skill. I've done this for so long I'm *good* at it." Which makes me wonder, do we get good at it because we are being biologically rewarded with our own chemical kickback, which brings us back to solitary pursuits for another shot of some inner opiate? If only couples were willing to do the work of being happily single (yes, it *is* work), would they feel the same? Can that be said for pining singles as well? Or are their brains so wired for oxytocin (or some other biological reward) that singlehood might just wind up feeling like being on welfare?

This question was highlighted for me recently when a fellow single gay friend was saying "It's hard to be on your own. You know what I mean," and I thought to myself, *no, not really.*

I *like* spending time by myself.

But just to be clear, none of this is intended to say that one's brain is 100 percent set, and that is it, one way or the other. One's needs and biochemistry change with age and experience. Getting through one's teens and twenties can leave one looking back in wonder at the circus of socialization of bars and mega bashes. And as many gay men turn thirty they enter into their more leisurely dinner-party years.

But certainly in the mind of one loner who is on a mission, there is no question that loners, like homosexuals, are born that way. Her name is Anneli Rufus, author of *Party of One: The Loners' Manifesto*.

The Loner

I stare at Rufus's book, a picture of a lone sheep on the cover, its frame small yet stoic amid what could be the Scottish Highlands. Ominous storm clouds billow overhead.

That gallant sheep is *so* me, though I'm more often compared to a goat.

Rufus grew up in what she calls the "loner land" of Los Angeles and after completing her English degree has pursued a career as a journalist.

"Sexuality's not a choice," she explains from her home in California. "You were born that way, and it's the same with loners. Some of us are born this way. We just can't do [groups], and that's OK." But then people feel bad about themselves because from a young age "people hammer it into your head that if you don't want to join, then you need to investigate your motives. Things done alone are regarded with suspicion and fear and pity compared to things done in groups, and that's why I wrote the book."

She talks about "the world at large," what she calls "the mob," and how it views singles.

"The presumption is if someone is by himself, what's wrong with him? Is he a loser, has he got PTSD (post-traumatic stress disorder) where someone dumped him and he can't get over it, or does he have some weird personal habit? There are so many assumptions people make about someone who is by himself. The last thing they think is he likes his own company. . . . That makes the single person seem healthy and good, and nobody wants to see that."

Having said that, Rufus is happily married, which some people think is cheating. "My answer is that people don't necessarily want to be by themselves their whole lives. You can't help falling in love, and my husband is also a loner, and we know how to work that."

And as Andrew Hostetler's research indicates, there are in fact gay men who maintain that they *like* being single, that they *prefer* it. Unfortunately, within a society that reveres the "mob," being alone is viewed with suspicion. As Rufus points out, to not have friends is seen as sad and pathetic, but to not *want* friends (or in this case a boyfriend) is perceived as monstrous, even serial-killerish.

But could it be that some of us really are just biochemically unsuited for long-term relationships?

Opiate Paradise vs. Boredom and Inertia

Writer, former gay activist, and self-professed love junkie Jeffrey Escoffier's description of himself marks him as a prime chemical candidate for long-term love. "In the long-term relationship that I had, the biggest surprise, which was not part of the shorter relationships, was after four years I began to experience this overwhelming deep pleasure over something I can only call domesticity. You sit at a table, not interacting but . . ." And his voice trails off, a look of remembered bliss overtaking his features. "That was to me one of the most amazing things, and talking to anybody in a long-term relationship, I'd say what is this? I didn't know this is what you got after four or five years, I was astonished by it, I loved it. Just sitting reading the morning paper and not talking to one another. All that taken for grantedness, for me that was a major thing you get from being in a long-term relationship. And a lot of people are just bored by that. I liked that. Nowadays I find tedious the energy and time required to develop a relationship. I'm not interested in that."

The feeling he describes is not as steep as the roller coaster of romantic love, but it is built to last, founded on friendship, familiarity, and affection. These are the rewards for making it through the dizzying (if intoxicating) phase of infatuation, which is often dominated by neediness, desperation, and anxiety.

The biological reward for sticking around after things like PEA and oxytocin wear off includes the "Attachment Chemical," a morphine-like opiate of the mind, which serves to calm and reassure. For many, this can be incredibly peaceful and healing. But not everyone reacts the same way. As Diane Ackerman points out, tedium can set in, and not everyone's looking for an opiate paradise—for some this leads to boredom and inertia.

Ultimately this creates an odd sort of dichotomy, one that has already been touched upon earlier in this book, and which other books on singlehood also mention. There is a push and pull between wanting to be with someone, and wanting to separate from them. Does one go with the PEA excitement of something new or the domestic bliss of what is known? Could some individuals be more chemically suited for one another? Are they mutually exclusive? Can they change over time? And what about those who aren't actively pursuing either?

There is, after all, a social-longing gray zone in which I believe the larger scope of love stands revealed.

I give you . . .

The Flirt Relationship

Whether one is a loner, a PEA junkie, or simply averse to domestic bliss, no discussion of the nature behind gay interactions is complete without looking at the potential biological basis of the all-important flirt relationship.

Sadly, this relationship often goes undervalued, in large part because homos have become obsessed with climbing a pair-based hierarchy of love. And yet in asking several gay men if they knew what I meant by a "flirt relationship," even "long-term flirt relationships," they all immediately said "absolutely." Sometimes these flirtations can go on for years.

"I am an admitted flirter," one man in his midthirties tells me. He's a clean-cut fellow and fits in well with his successful preppy crowd.

"So what do you get out of it?" I ask.

"Sometimes not much, which is upsetting considering how much effort actually goes into it." Then he reconsiders. "You know, after being out of the closet for fifteen years, it's actually not that much effort. It's kind of like peeing."

Flirting needs a closer look, in its natural habitat.

We Are Not Just Homosexuals, We Are Homosociables

It's a Thursday night at Toronto's stand-and-model gay bar Woody's. A throng of gay men cheer for their favorite shirtless contestants as the Best Chest Contest gets into full swing. But the real show's happening offstage. A crush/flirt friend of many years finally has his hand down the back of my pants for the first time.

His finger is wedged in the top of my crack, drawing my crotch closer to his while our postures relax toward each other, without actually touching. The feeling is not just sexual. It is overwhelmingly friendly. As I look about the bar, at the touches exchanged by friends, exes, and potential paramours, I wonder if we should change our label from "homosexuals" to "homo*sociables*."

Much of this touching is not about sex per se. Don't get me wrong. People are testing the waters for potential encounters. But amid the angst and attitude, the posing and sometimes abrasive cruising, there is a tactile sociability here, a sexual *playfulness*.

I know what I am going to propose will sound more like science fiction than science, but so be it. Perhaps it's even appropriate that it falls into the realm of speculative fiction, an homage to those queers who, in the '20s and '30s, would surreptitiously correspond through personal columns in sci-fi newsletters. As Susan Stryker writes in *Queer Pulp*, "the genre was exceptionally well-suited to extrapolate from contemporary social concerns and promote visions of alternative societies, new forms of embodiment, and novel pathways for desire and pleasure."

And that's exactly what I'm going to explore: novel pathways for desire and pleasure. Flirtation is not just a means to an end but at times an end unto itself, one that takes wanting to be with someone, but not wanting to stay with them, to a whole new level.

Homosocially Enabled

From an evolutionary point of view, homosexuality is a paradox.

At least on the surface.

In *A Natural History of Love* Diane Ackerman surmises that heterosexual love has given humans a survival advantage and that it is a biological imperative.

"Just as evolution favored human beings who were able to stand upright, it favored human beings who felt love. It favored them because love has great survival value. Those who felt love made sure their offspring survived, those offspring inherited the ability to love, and they lived longer and had more offspring of their own."

But she was speaking specifically of the love between a man and woman engaged in procreation and rearing. This has long been a quandary for biological theories on homosexuality. Gay sex distracts from procreative sex, and those who primarily have the urge to mate with the same sex would definitely not be passing on their genes to nearly the same extent (gay men are estimated to produce 80 percent fewer offspring than heteros), so should not natural selection have stamped homos out?

Not if they in some way contribute to survival.

Perhaps homosexuality in and of itself does not do so, at least not directly, but homo*sociability* is a different story, and homosociability does indeed appear to have a genetic link, one that might be connected to homo*sexuality*.

And flirting, particularly in gay culture, is as much about socializing as it is about sexualizing.

"I love flirting," says one man. "It sustains me."

So where does this same-sex sociability fit into increased survivability for an individual to pass on the same-sex flirt genes? Could this be the very reason gay men exist? As a by-product of straight men's social attraction for each other? As one psychologist friend of mine pointed out, "straight men and women generally don't even like each other. The only reason they spend time together is because of sex. Do you know what you call a man who actually likes hanging out with women? Gay."

When looked at closely, love starts to get very muddled indeed. Instead of recognizing this complexity, gays have unfortunately (if understandably) become so obsessed with rights, in a society that caters to the pair-bonded, that we have taken a very narrow interpretation of the nature of love. Gays have long turned to biology to justify our existence as natural and to find equality have become a bit obsessed with fitting every gay individual into a pair-bonded model. But love can't easily be broken down into lifetime pair bonds between individual men and women, or between one man and another, especially when one starts to look at homosociability on a genetic level.

Fruity the Fly

In *Time, Love, Memory,* Pulitzer Prize–winning evolution writer Jonathan Weiner chronicles the search for the origins of behavior. He details a series of studies that took place in a slew of test tubes and other bottles full of fruit flies. Male fruit flies would get irradiated to see what behaviors might get messed up by scrambling their genes with X-rays, and thus researchers could look at which behaviors were genetically linked. Among the results of these experiments were a series of mutant male fruit flies that displayed a range of courtship challenges.

There was a fellow who'd woo with great gusto but never copulate. He was dubbed *celibate*. Then there was the little guy who'd pull out after ten minutes or so of pumping. He rarely fathered any offspring and was named *coitus interruptus*. In another lab there arose the nightmare of all men: *stuck*, which struggled to withdraw from the female after a good shag. They could pull for hours, even days, sometimes starving to death as a result of the failure to separate.

In 1963, a group of male flies was discovered that had little interest in copulation at all, and which displayed other non-normative gender behavior. Normally in the bustle of fruit fly life confined to a test tube, when two males bump into each other they'll retreat a few steps and start grooming themselves. And in general, if a male sees another male approaching in a manner consistent with courting, such as extending a wing outward, it will flick its own wings like a grade-A stud lounging in his bathhouse cubicle waving away some fatherly troll.

Not so with these male mutants. They would actually *sing* to each other. In all other procreative manners they were sexually quite up to snuff, tests showing that their sperm was healthy and they would even court females, wooing them with great gusto—but no follow-through.

Seduction, yes.

Boom boom, no.

Researchers believed they'd found the "quintessential courtship gene."

Pussy tease gene is more like it, but here's where things get *really* gay.

"Sometimes three males, or five, ten, or more would form chains and follow each other around in the fly bottle in long, winding conga lines," writes Weiner. "They would chain for hours. They tended to stay down around the food at the bottom of a bottle, but when the dancing had reached a certain pitch of frenzy they would get right up onto the glass walls of the bottle and chain. Often they broke up and then came back together. They took little breathing spaces and went right back to chaining."

The males made no attempt to copulate with each other, and as one technician noted, it looked like some sort of *social* thing. Sociability among fruit flies? Shut up.

Weiner describes the scene this way: "In Dante's vision of the tenth circle of Hell, sodomites go round and round with their bodies linked in a wheel, circling on burnt sand in a whirl of ever-moving feet. In [this] Fly Room, the scene looked like Dante's. The male mutant flies whirled in bottles and Petri dishes and test tubes—long swirling sinuous chains, males only, winding their way around and around, hour after hour."

Throw in a few hits of E and a good Hex Hector remix and you've got a circuit party (as my friend Parker observed recently at a local gay party night, "I'm looking for sex, but a lot of these guys are here *socializing*.")

The investigator at Yale named the mutant *fruity*. Another later renamed it *fruitless*.

In 1989 researchers tracked down what was happening on a genetic level. The X-rays that the flies had been zapped with had popped out a piece of DNA. When it was repaired, it got put back in backward.

An inversion.

Granted, it was artificially catalyzed by X-rays, but inversions do occur in nature, and an inversion on the *courtship* gene suddenly led to male fruit flies being drawn to each other, en masse, and not in a sexual way per se, but in a *social* way.

It is an amazing example of the potential genetics behind male same-sex attraction, one that in this case has little to do with pair-bonding for life. Having said that, fruit flies and humans are, to say the least, quite different, so let's look at the closest relatives of humans, and how this kind of same-sex social behavior might be playing out in another species.

Grooming Leads to Power

"Throughout the societies of monkeys, cooperation is encountered almost exclusively in the context of competition and aggression. It is, in male monkeys, a way of winning fights," writes Matt Ridley in *The Origins of Virtue,* pointing to the way junior males get to have sex by teaming up and beating a senior male to get to his monopoly of females. "Two weak individuals, by cooperating, can beat a stronger one. What counts is not strength but social skills. . . . The well-connected will inherit the earth."

Baboons form occasional but stable alliances. Best friends, if you will.

But the bonnet macaques, a ground-dwelling monkey, form alliances frequently, and they are ever shifting.

"Every male in the troop will at some time form a coalition with every other male. Male bonding is not confined to the odd head-flagging precursor to a battle; it is the stuff of life. Males groom each other, play with each other, huddle together, snooze in each other's arms, wander about in pairs and generally spend vast amounts of effort creating and maintaining temporary friendships with each other. . . . On average, males support males that have supported them or groomed them in the past and, on average, rank plays a big role: supporters in fights are usually senior males coming to the aid of junior ones. Junior ones return the compliment by grooming their senior allies."

I'm not saying any of the above are sexual exchanges in any way, but it does imply some sort of bond, however temporary, forged from male physical contact.

Chimpanzees provide a variation on this theme. They are among humanity's closest relatives and are known as the politicians of the primate world because of the key role social adeptness plays in their power structure. The alpha male garners support by sharing food with other males in the middle of the power structure, forging allegiances against the more powerful males who might threaten him at some point. Allowing access to females is another bartering chip.

But when it comes time to rally the troops, for instance to defend territory, chimps work to rouse their friends by holding out a hand or embracing them. What's interesting here is that they defend the territory against other males of other troops, group against group as opposed to individual against individual, and the preparation for this group physical violence is precipitated by what could be described as male-male physical bonding among allies.

Who knew flirting could be so powerful and useful—not to

achieve sex, in this instance, but to forge social cohesion. I bring this up because in our own interactions we are very quick to dismiss any kind of social relation as "just" this or "just" that unless it lasts forever. And yet even in some of the shortest and seemingly modest of sociosexual interactions, there is a miracle of biology at play, and we should stand in awe of it.

But I understand why we minimize these moments of light flirtation within gay culture: sometimes we think the flirtation is leading to sex and/or a date and are disappointed, perhaps even feeling led on when it doesn't.

I know that I am not alone in emerging from an intense flirtation that goes no further wondering, "What was that all about? Was I just feeding someone's ego all this time?"

Sometimes, maybe. There are flirtations I either initiate or encourage when I myself just want to reassure myself that I've "still got it."

But there are other moments when I realize, *I'm enjoying this other person's company, his touch, our interplay of words, even though I have no need or desire to get naked with him.*

I am enjoying his short-term company, this casual pseudo-physical bond, and that is enough.

Wanting to be with him is natural. Not wanting to stay with him is, too.

Maries in the Mist

Perhaps the greatest inspiration and example of the utility of same-sex flirtations within a social context is the bonobo, "lover" of the primate world, with which we share about 98 percent of our DNA. As in humans, the female's sexual anatomy is situated toward the front of the body, and penetrative sex between males and females often involves frontal entry and face-to-face encounters, with lots of staring into each other's eyes. They also engage in sex for pleasure, in a range of positions that would do the Kama Sutra proud, including open-mouthed kissing with lots of tongue play.

"Whereas in most other species, sexual behavior is a fairly distinct category," says Dr. Franz de Waal in *Bonobo: The Forgotten Ape*, "in the bonobo it has become an integral part of social relationships, and not just between males and females. Bonobos engage in sex in virtually every partner combination: male-male, male-female, female-female, male-juvenile, female-juvenile, and so on."

But he notes that these encounters are brief, and between males does not involve ejaculation, taking on a tone that's more casual than sexual. The purpose seems to be to diffuse tension before it can result in violence. Not that they don't fight, but they do so less frequently than other primates, and sexual contact is often a method of reconciliation when disputes do occur.

I think of the times when an acquaintance's light touch would put me at ease and make me feel accepted within a group. And let's not forget makeup sex.

De Waal recounts one scenario involving two males who were not getting along,

"Both males had erections, which they presented to each other with legs apart, in the same way that a male invites a female for sex. It was as if each male wanted contact but did not know whether the other could be trusted. When they finally did rush towards each other, instead of fighting, they embraced frontally with broad grins on their faces, Vernon thrusting his genitals against Kevin's. They calmed down right away and happily began collecting the raisins that the caretakers had scattered around.

"The chimpanzee tries to gain influence and get the upper hand, whereas the bonobo follows a less power-hungry scheme. After all, there are many ways to get what one wants. . . . The chimpanzee resolves sexual issues with power; the bonobo resolves power issues with sex."

Now, when he says sex between males, he is not referring to anal penetration. But even among the sexual encounters of gay men, anal penetration is not assumed, and one study found that gay men's preferred sexual behavior, in order of preference, were masturbation, oral sex, kissing and body rubbing, with anal intercourse surprisingly coming in fourth, alongside massage.

Back to Woody's

I keep the bonobos in mind as I stand with a work acquaintance at Woody's. The guy who had his hand down the back of my pants is across the bar talking with some other friends of his. As various acquaintances pass by they touch me, I touch them, hand on hip, palm on belly, lip to passing cheek, we share a superficial laugh, sometimes without even really hearing what the other has said. I'm not saying this is the deepest of bonds. For the most part, these are not people who would visit me in the hospital if I were sick, or even come to my funeral, nor vice versa. But the interaction is an important one, as the words of my colleague make clear.

"You just reach out and touch this one, kiss that one," he says, his tone one of such wonder and disbelief that it brings me back to a time when I could not just reach out and kiss this one or touch that one, when I first moved to the city and felt outside of this mass where everyone seemed to know everyone, except me. On the outside they all seemed to be the closest of friends. Now that I'd made my way in, I realized they were the closest of acquaintances. I have seen the same dynamic play out in almost any gay gathering, from bars to circuit parties to cocktail parties to brunch to walking down a gay strip on a summer day, when the fags stand outside Starbucks or Timothy's and just hang out sipping their lattes.

For the most part all this touching is not leading to sex, but it does lead to a sense of inclusion that lasts beyond the moment, and the tactile experience can be both exciting and soothing at the same time. Sometimes I go out just for that, or just to be among gay men, even if I don't run into anyone I know. Apparently I can be a loner and social at the same time.

And this brings us back to those chemical pathways discussed earlier that give us the feeling of romantic love, or the cuddle chemical, or the opiates of comfort.

The Drug of Friendship

I can't help but wonder if there's some connection between these molecules and human bonding in general, and for the purposes of this book, male bonding in particular. In humans it's been demonstrated that PEA doesn't just play a role in sex but also rises when we are in new and unfamiliar environments.

The biological pathways for love and stress are the *same*, and PEA has been shown to rise during exercise. Natural selection doesn't just invent new pathways, it recycles old ones, favoring preexisting ones if they wind up having fringe benefits, increasing the presence of such traits through the gene pool. Perhaps PEA originally served to bring men and women together for mating, but could it have come to play a part in team bonding, on the football field for instance, where cooperation within a group of aggressive males requires that individuals within that team focus their aggression not on each other but instead act as one against the opposing team?

The frequent ass smacking that's part of the ritual is pretty scanty evidence, but it is often referred to in discussions of homoerotic undercurrents in sports and the army, where homosexuality can be fiercely reviled, in part because it "ruins" the otherwise "innocent" physical bonding between males that is integral to the team. These guys may very well be arousing each other (though not necessarily turning each other on) through this shared activity, and thus forming a sociosexual chemical bond of solidarity.

I offer this as a contemporary example of what I envision during more primitive times (though I'm not sure if you can get much more primitive than a bunch of grown men jumping all over each other for a blown-up piece of pig skin or trying to blow each other up), when a group of primates would fare better than one alone (especially if that one alone comes up against a group), and so would need some inheritable, possibly chemical reward if this were a behaviorally predisposed cooperative trait.

"Male chimpanzees . . . hunt together, engage in warfare over territory, and enjoy a half-amicable, half-competitive camaraderie. Their cooperative, action-packed existence resembles that of the human males who, in modern society, team up with other males in corporations," says de Waal.

He should do a study on Woody's.

I pause for a moment to think of all the circuit parties I've been to, of these warehouse spaces filled with gay men, and although there was drama to be had, rarely was there any physical violence. Take the exact same space bursting with a mix of straight men and women, and not only are there fights but security frisks for weapons, and at some venues patrons walk through a metal detector. During gay events at the identical locale, it's give your ticket and start to party. That's pretty crazy and incredible.

I think again of a quote by Dr. Franz de Waal in *Bonobo: The Forgotten Ape.*

"The chimpanzee resolves sexual issues with power; the bonobo resolves power issues with sex."

In humans, too, sex and sexuality bring us together for more than getting off, and for reasons other than pairing up for a lifetime. The desire to be with someone is natural. Not wanting—or needing—to remain in that state forever is, too.

You Can Find Intimacy and Emotional Growth *Without* a Boyfriend

If you are single, after graduation there isn't one occasion where people celebrate you. . . . Hallmark doesn't make a Congratulations, You Didn't Get Married to the Wrong Guy card.

—Carrie Bradshaw (aka Sarah Jessica Parker),
Sex and the City

I'VE NEVER HAD A boyfriend, but I've definitely had breakups. The most intense was with Vance, my best friend of many, many years. Vance and I really bonded in our early twenties when we ran into each other at gay day at Canada's Wonderland, an amusement park outside of Toronto. I was there because I had a crush on one of the organizers and was hoping our paths would cross. He was there with a friend who he'd ditched because the friend wasn't into roller coasters. In other words, we were both there alone, and as we discovered, going on a ride alone is not as much fun as going on it with someone else.

Our friendship has been a lot like the roller-coaster rides we shared that day, with lots of ups, downs, and upside downs, the pair of us screaming like teenage girls loving the fearful adrenaline of it all; until things went raging off track.

As in many gay friendships, emotional lines got blurred, and as discussed earlier, it is within this gray zone that many gay men come into their emotional adulthood, rather than "growing up" by getting married. But what lies beyond that? Whatever I might say about the naturalness of the single state, and the amorphous affections that I believe are part of our biological makeup, is the intimacy each person needs available for the single gay man within an often helter-skelter culture? Maybe friendship isn't enough. After all, there are studies that indicate a commitment such as marriage can make one's life healthier and less filled with anxiety because of the calming belief that someone is there for you. And some therapists would go further and say that long-term boyfriend-style relationships can help us grow and heal childhood wounds by breaking old patterns based on how we related to our parents.

If I am to be honest, I must admit this sometimes makes me worry that I am in fact missing out on something by not being in a boyfriend-style relationship, especially as I dig deeper into what a boyfriend might (emphasis on *might*) provide.

Broken Boys and the Oedipal Complex

In the previous chapter I pushed the idea that wanting to be with someone is natural, and not wanting to stay with him is, too. But as I explored the biology of desire and where homosexuality might fit into that, I avoided getting into the impact of nurture on our nature. In humans, one can't really be separated from the other. After all, we emerge from the womb with our brains only partially formed. Our neural pathways are largely undeveloped, and it is within this still maturing brain that we are flooded with endorphins when we are hugged and held. This neurotransmitter fills the body with a feeling of happiness and security. The first few years of life are critical in laying down this circuitry, which will determine in large part what kind of emotional lives we will lead as adults.

More specifically, it is when babies learn to equate affection with pleasure.

But much can go awry in this process, and some believe that gay men are at higher risk of "faulty" electrical work.

For heterosexuals, Freud's Oedipus complex describes a young boy's erotic desire for his mother as part of his psychosexual development, and a consequent hatred, even a desire for the death, of his father, who is perceived as a barrier to the mother.

In his book *Being Homosexual*, psychotherapist Dr. Richard

Isay theorizes a similar mechanism at work for gay men, one with long-term consequences in the search for intimacy in adulthood.

He says it became clear to him from working with adult gay men that although most of them say their homoerotic attraction started somewhere between the ages of eight and fourteen, "homoerotic fantasies are usually present from at least the ages of four or five years. This period of development is analogous to the Oedipal stage in heterosexual boys, except that the primary sexual object of homosexual boys is their fathers."

He believes it is these same-sex erotic desires focused on the father that make us feel different from our peers. Gay boys may also develop "feminine" mannerisms by mimicking one's mother figure as a way of attracting the father's love and attention, much as hetero boys will model themselves after their father to gain Mama's attention.

Isay believes that this atypical behavior can lead to these boys experiencing paternal and peer rejection, thus developing a sense of being an outsider, and can result in unhappiness and further isolation, as well as excessive emotionality.

"Defenses against these erotic feelings may lead to a distortion of the gay man's perception of other men and to a fear of intimacy and may be the most important psychological cause of inhibited and impoverished relations in adulthood," says Isay.

He bases his findings on what his gay patients have told him during therapy, which he admits is not a random sample, and may only apply to those who feel the need to seek out therapy. Still, his observations do provide an interesting framework for how at least some gay men develop from early childhood and the impact peer rejection and fatherly rejection can have on their ability to trust later in life and form intimate relationships with men.

Some avoid intimacy altogether, others embark on the journey of love extremely guardedly and fully anticipate further rejection. Others may form "spite and revenge" attachments without even realizing it, rejecting partners as compensation for having been rejected in childhood.

In the experience of therapist Joe Kort, "far too many gay men enter love relationships with the unspoken, internalized conviction that they're inherently damaged and flawed." And then they play out the same scripts in adulthood, seeking out people who remind them of the characters of Mommy and Daddy from their past, often choosing "exits" rather than working through the uncomfortable emotions this will inevitably churn up.

Wow.

That's really depressing. Kind of takes the wind out of my "gay and single is good" sails, but only a bit, and only for a moment.

In conversation, Kort is quick to clarify his position, saying that he frequently sees single gay men struggling not with finding love in their life but with being OK with the love that they already have.

"They're in close relationships with their mother or a female friend or a gay best friend," he says, "so there's no reason to have a partner. They say they want a partner because that's what they're supposed to say, but it's OK to say I get that from my friend or my mother, and that's enough."

But is it really?

In his extremely insightful book *10 Smart Things Gay Men Can Do to Improve Their Lives*, Joe Kort includes "commit to a partner" on his top-ten list.

"Our deepest healing as individuals—and especially as gay men—is achieved in a committed adult love relationship." He argues that not committing provides an easy exit from relationship situations that challenge the individual, possibly even creating anxiety by dredging up old childhood hurts and wounds, which, if worked out, would help the individual grow.

The Friendship Breakup

From riding roller coasters, Vance and I went to calling each other three times a day, and our friendship became more like a codependent marriage, right down to the complete lack of sex with each other. We had little need or desire to socialize with anyone else in any meaningful way, to the point where I think we both knew we'd gotten ourselves into an emotional pressure cooker that was bound to blow. But we liked each other so much we turned a blind eye to building trouble and hoped for the best.

It was a trick of mine that finally popped the lid. Vance was sleeping in my spare room while visiting from out of town. The trick and I were making out on the couch in the living room, trapping Vance in the spare room when he needed to go the bathroom.

When it was finally safe for him to come out, he heard the inevitable sounds of sex echoing from my bedroom.

The next day, with no plausible explanation for an early departure, Vance was booking himself on the first train back to Montreal.

I didn't know it at the time, but it was the beginning of our breakup.

So why was *this* the proverbial straw?

It's not that we didn't know about each other's sex lives. On the contrary, talking about sex was part of the glue of our camaraderie. We'd compare notes on one-night stands and bathhouse escapades over toaster waffles the next morning. But this was different. This was not a story. This was happening in real time. And that, as he later explained, was too much, too in his face. The feelings provoked by hearing his best friend having sex with another guy made him realize that he didn't want a sexless make-believe marriage anymore.

There was a bittersweet irony. I was the one constantly on the prowl for a potential boyfriend. After a bad past relationship, Vance wanted nothing to do with one. And yet because of our love for each other—and we most definitely were a couple in all ways but one—he found himself wanting the friendship to involve romance. I felt like a failure for not feeling able to step up to the plate.

The angry emails back and forth ended in each of us saying to the other that we needed time apart.

Was this an "exit" or could commitment have been the answer?

Intimacy, Commitment, and Healing

When Vance and I broke up, and it was a breakup, I felt that a part of my heart had been literally ripped out. It's as if there were an empty hole deep in my chest and it ached day after day after day.

And there were many times when I just started freaking out.

When Vance would come to visit I loved it that he'd clean my floors and do my dishes, but when our LTR ended I retroactively took this kindness as a slap in the face, as if he was saying I couldn't take care of myself. I went on a rampage of mopping and dusting, replacing the garbage bag over one window with an actual curtain, having new throw pillows made from the excess material.

I'd show him.

Thankfully, in time, the hole in my chest slowly filled, and the freak-outs became fewer and farther between (for Vance, too, even if he did burn the *Ab Fab* videocassettes I'd given him for his birthday—"I didn't know plastic gave off so much smoke," he told me years later).

In the meanwhile, I made some new friends, became closer

with some existing ones, and for a while I got into the party scene that had long held an allure for me, and which held little interest for Vance. In this scene, I got to pursue those muscle boys I'd long been afraid to go after and touch, unless they were a stripper that I was paying for lap dances at ten dollars a song.

Perhaps this was the dreaded "delayed adolescence" rearing its head, but if so I needed to go through it. If one of the benefits of having a boyfriend is working through shit from our youth, including peer rejection, in this milieu I got a chance to play with my peers and feel, as my pal Parker once put it, "like one of the boys."

I look back on those days with an odd nostalgia. I had my party posse, with my kissing friend/dance-off partner, as well as a straight bud and his girlfriend, not to mention their various friends, and of course at the center of our clique, the "taste tester," so-called because he'd tried all the various tablets of E (each of which had its own name based on its color and the image stamped into it) before any of us had, and could tell us what kind of high a hit of "green apple" or "pink Mercedes" would give.

I favored lovey dovey over anything with too much speed.

That seems like a different life now, just as high school does. I still go out. I still go to parties, but my drug use has steadily decreased as the negative come downs have steadily increased, to the point where recreational drugs hold little to no appeal.

Still, I think about some of the grander evenings from that time of my life, the way someone might reminisce about prom night. When I look back there are a couple of things that I take with me out of the experience. One, instead of feeling like I have to break into this scene the way I wanted to break into the cool kid cliques in high school, I now feel free to step in and out rather than believing I'm being excluded.

Two, I feel that whatever emotional maturing and healing Vance and I were going to do, for us anyway, the first step was disentangling ourselves from each other. As with many a long-term relationship we'd fallen into the trap of sloppy enmeshment.

There's a Difference Between a Healthy Relationship and a Codependent Relationship

During the course of my research I picked up a book with a title so cheesy I almost decided to order it online rather than face a cashier at the checkout counter. It's called *The Authentic Heart: An Eightfold Path to Midlife Love,* written by Dr. John Amodeo, a counselor for more than twenty years and also the author of *Love & Betrayal,* and *Being Intimate.* He has much to say on "sloppy enmeshment."

His focus is very much on couplehood, straight couplehood, but his writing sucked me in, highlighter in hand, for a couple of reasons.

"Although life can be richer with a loving partnership, it's liberating to realize that you can create a satisfying life without a mate," he writes. "Instead of narrowing your options by pursuing 'The Relationship,' you can increase them by developing a network of meaningful connections." And he emphasizes that "if you're unwilling to stand alone, you may seek companionship that offers no real intimacy. You might hold on to a relationship that's toxic to your well-being. Fearful of losing something that you never really had, you may go through the motions of having a relationship, when no real 'relating' is happening."

He warns against "sloppy enmeshment" and insists that true intimacy involves a "curious paradox," in that boundaries and autonomy are essential to prevent simply becoming what one thinks the other person wants, instead of remaining true to one's self.

I believe that the years Vance and I spent apart were key for us to rediscover our own identities. Only then were we able to start growing and growing up, on our own, and then with each other. In fact I had to relearn how to be alone, and in the words of Amodeo, how to practice "self-soothing" and ride out uncomfortable feelings without trying to suppress them or turning to someone to distract me from myself.

Not Just an Exit, Also an Entrance

All the same, it was with great joy that after several years my friendship with Vance resumed with a simple email from out of the blue.

Hey Steven, I saw you at Pride a few weeks ago. I wanted to say hi. If you don't want to e-mail me back, I understand, but I thought it would be nice to be in touch.

We've been friends again ever since, on much more honest terms.

It has been said that a gay person does not have a true friend until he comes out, for only then does he let his true self be seen. And for a gay man who's fallen for a gay friend, that friendship can no longer be true until that love is put on the table, for again, to lie about what one feels and thinks on such a core level is to lie about one's true self.

Interestingly, Vance is now the one who is openly seeking a relationship.

"You made me realize it was possible to feel love again," he told me.

And I'm more honest with myself about what I'm really looking for.

"You made me realize it's OK to be slutty," I told him.

So beyond our sloppy enmeshment, we've found honesty and our own separate selves. And yes, there is commitment within this kind of long-term relationship, as I have learned. If we were ever to break up again, which now that we are in our thirties, I really don't see happening, I know it wouldn't last, and our friendship definitely would.

Still, there's no ring, no ceremony, no walk down the aisle or exchanging vows in front of friends or family, so can I really be getting as much out of this as someone would from the sense of committing through marriage?

All I can honestly say in terms of me and Vance "lasting" is that we've now been through enough storms to know there's usually a calm that lies beyond it. And another storm beyond that. One that I have faith I can weather, as can our friendship. At the end of the day, it is this sense of faith that can provide health benefits to couples who have made a commitment to each other, because there is a belief that someone will be there for you, which serves as a means of soothing one's worries, and reduces the negative effects that can come with stress.

But in the words of one sixty-year-old gay man I interviewed, "We should say *just* a boyfriend, because the friendship lasts longer."

As Vance put it to me when he found out I was going to be writing about our breakup, "you better include that that guy so wasn't worth it." He is beyond right. To me this realization is a form of commitment, and to me this is soothing, much more so than my attempts at boyfriendship.

In fact, with the amount of psychological pressure I used to put on myself to get a guy, I'm sure a study on me alone would show that I was better off with a boyfriend—'cause I could finally let myself relax (unless of course I was freaking out about how to go about keeping him, how not to let him see my faults, and most especially how not to pass wind in front of him.)

So at the end of the day, I find myself not so worried about studies showing couples are happier and have improved health over singles. After all, this isn't *all* couples, and this isn't *all* singles, just averages. There's overlap either way.

With that in mind I am delighted to cheerlead Vance in his quest for a suitable mate.

"You can do your whole gay and single forever thing, but I want a husband," he tells me. As for myself, I am taking a different path for my own continued growth beyond my delayed adolescence. I'm not saying this route is better, nor that it is for everyone, but relationship pressure has made me neurotic for too long and so, like many other longtime singles, my life is taking a developmental course outside the "normal" trajectory.

The Life Course

The model for the so-called ideal life is laid down for us as if it were a series of steps that must be taken in a specific linear sequence, and which must be mastered on our route to full adulthood. From grade school to elementary school to high school to some sort of post-secondary education to gainful employment, then marriage, house, and kids, it's a pretty straightforward blueprint.

However, many longtime singles have come to reject it. A study of mature singles done by Statistics Canada found that half of that country's 1.1 million mature singles (over twenty-eight years old for women, thirty for men) did not expect to marry because they had "less conventional views about the importance of love, marriage and family."

In other words, they were following a different story, likely one based on their own opinions and life experiences. This comes back to the narrative solution discussed by Andrew Hostetler. It also marks a developmental and growth process of the maturing single, and a way of regaining a sense of control and balance in one's life.

Here's how it works.

Primary vs. Secondary Control

"From a cultural perspective," Andrew Hostetler tells me, "the way North Americans think about choice is we think about bringing the external environment in line with what we want." This is known as "primary control." But "secondary choice is about conforming to reality, assimilating to an extent to reality while still salvaging a sense of self-esteem."

Applied to relationships, primary control in a relationship-centric world would be to get a boyfriend. This would change one's scenario by conforming to what is perceived as ideal. Secondary control would be to accept singlehood and I guess make the best of it, which sounds an awful lot like a cop-out as opposed to a step toward developmental growth.

But a friend made an interesting comparison between this and working out. He's got a choice: he can become comfortable with his skinny body, or he can do something about changing it. But the idea of going to the gym and eating lots of food really does not appeal to him. Regardless of what he decides, it will be a developmental stage for him. Maybe going to the gym and eating a bit more would be good for him. Maybe it will become more of an obsession that winds up controlling him more than the other way around. Maybe that's another growth stage he goes through before settling into a more healthy and grounded relationship between himself, the gym, and his body. Or maybe he'll take a look in the mirror, or forget the fucking mirror, and accept himself as he is. This is secondary control, as he changes his mind instead of his body to achieve a sense of personal agency.

Even when it comes to getting into a relationship, primary control is overrated. All the gay relationship books I've read focus on changing one's expectations at least a little to adapt to the reality of what having a boyfriend is really like, and they urge readers to reevaluate their criteria for a potential mate (i.e., ripped abs is apparently not the best guarantee of compatibility, and even if it were, one should still expect disagreements along the way. Maybe he'll prefer strawberry protein shakes and for you it's vanilla all the way. Who can say?). Either way, adaptation to the environment at hand is going to be required, so the question partly becomes what will be your own balance between primary and secondary control.

In applying this to boyfriends and singlehood, I remember telling my former therapist that I wasn't looking for a boyfriend but that a fuck buddy would be great.

"It sounds like that's a way of taking the pressure off" was his response.

I think he's right, and having the pressure off of feeling like I have to change my environment is such a fucking relief. I'm not sure if there's a single's equivalent to body dismorphia, but if there is, I think secondary control might be the way out of outgrowing it.

God bless.

The Man I Might Become

Most of the stories I've related from my personal life in this chapter took place from my mid to late twenties, and I do fear that it may be too laden with tales of sex and occasional drug use for everyone to identify with. Or perhaps there's not enough sex and drug use for others to identify with. Not every gay man gets into partying as part of a delayed adolescence. Some don't get into at all. And not everyone leaves partying behind as part of their maturation (although nowadays if you're messy at a party you're seen as an amateur). At any rate, my point with these tales is that shit happens, to all of us, and whatever that shit happens to be it hopefully helps us grow into better people.

Now that I'm in my early thirties, I wonder what shit still lies ahead on this nonlinear spiral of growth that some believe is the pattern for many longtime singles. There is of course the dreaded vision of the lonely old queen, which has long been used as part of the conspiracy against homosexuality and singlehood. With its hints of psychosexual pathology, this vision is even more fearsome than that of the lonely old maid.

But there are alternative story lines to the archetype of the sexually predatory aging homosexual.

In *Gay and Gray: The Older Homosexual Man*, Raymond M.

Berger did a study of a little more than one hundred gay men forty-one to seventy-seven years old, living in a mix of urban, suburban, and semirural locales. He found that in general they were better able to meet the challenges of old age than their heterosexual counterparts because of the "mastery of crisis" hypotheses. "The older homosexual typically faces the crisis of independence much earlier, and he cannot usually look to a family of procreation for support. . . . Because the crisis of independence must be resolved in young adulthood, his transition to old age and retirement is often less severe."

As in other studies, Berger also found older gay men were no more likely to be isolated or lonely than their younger counterparts, continuing to date and 75 percent reporting satisfaction with their sex lives. Many of them lived with a roommate, a family member, or a lover.

But there are some potential developmental shifts along the way, including the gay midlife crisis.

"At midlife we gradually separate from our identity as a boy or a younger man," writes clinical social worker Rik Insensee in one of his many books on gay men, *Are You Ready?: The Gay Man's Guide to Thriving at Midlife.* "We begin to reassess possibilities in the face of personal limitations."

By midlife he means one's forties and fifties, where among other things one is faced with an aging body and changing looks, the deaths of parents, and the reminder of one's own pending mortality. Primary control becomes ever more elusive in several arenas and can actually spawn forms of evasion, from chronic plastic surgery to bitter drinking as one fights to retain one's appearance and social standing (I still want a facelift when I get older). "We tend to see external change as the answer, whereas the 'answer' may reveal itself through an internal shift in perspective," writes Insensee.

Sounds like secondary control to me.

New Focuses

Beyond a greater acceptance of one's own limitations, there can also be a refocusing of priorities at midlife. As one man in Insensee's book comments, "At midlife the question is no longer 'What do I want to be when I grow up?' It's 'What do I want to have accomplished before I die?'"

"When I was young I thought I had to be in a relationship all the time," sixty-two-year-old Jeffrey Escoffier tells me during one of several conversations. His first sexual liaison was with his sister's boyfriend when he was sixteen, an experience he repeated with another of her beaus. "When my sister broke up with them, I lost them, too." But in truth, "I never felt like they were truly mine. Still, for a while I thought that's how I would meet a boyfriend. I'd encourage guys I was attracted to to go after my sister."

In college he fell in love with the love of his life, a man he's still friends with. Since then he's had several relationships, including one that lasted eight years. But this self-avowed "love slut," who finds he just can't do one-night stands, has now been single since 1992. "I loved falling in love. I was addicted to that. Even when I was in a relationship I was always falling in love with other people. But there is a choice at some point. I used to spend a lot of my time looking for relationships, and I don't do it anymore."

He feels that time's now running out on him, and he's focusing his attention on unfinished business, and unrealized dreams. Over the years he's been an activist and an editor, working for *The Socialist Review*, starting up the queer national magazine *Out/Look*, and founding Philadelphia's Gay Activist Alliance in the '70s. But the truth is, he's always wanted to be a writer.

"I've had lots of sex in my life, lots of relationships of one sort or another, and right now this is the most important thing to me. I always wanted to write. I never wrote, and now I'm doing it, and that's what I care about. I'm not totally happy, and I get nostalgic for relationships every now and then, and I feel like I'm in a rush. I spent most of my life working at marginal political activist things. I edited a socialist publication for eight years, started another publication for another five years, and now I have no money. So I work now for the New York Health Department. I have a pension. I have health benefits. So I feel, OK . . . if I want to write, I have to spend the rest of my life doing that."

It's strange for me to hear his story, because growing up single, in the depths of my worst wanna have a boyfriend angst, I'd stop my downward spiral and put it in perspective by asking myself: *If I had to choose between a boyfriend and a book deal, which would I pick?*

Writing had always been there for me.

Boys had not.

Writing helped me build self-esteem and dare to dream and allowed me a safe outlet during my teen years, when I was otherwise emotionally shut down.

Boys were torture.

The dream of having a book published won hands down, and it brought me great comfort to know that the writing was more important to me, for this was within my control and made me feel that I had a central purpose in life. I just never expected the universe to honor my bargain with myself in such a literal way, as demonstrated by the book you are reading, my first to be published.

The more I speak with men like Escoffier, the more I see possibilities for my own developmental course as a single gay man.

Tricksters, Shamans, and Healers

One of these men that I've become friends with is sixty-six-year-old author Wayson Choy, and in him I see what Rik Insensee would called the wise "shaman" or "trickster" figure, who can act as a healer for the younger set in their wiser years. There is something so gentle in Wayson Choy's voice, just listening to him tell a story, any story, from ghost tales to suffering a near fatal asthma attack to his most wonderful night at the baths many years ago, one is caught up in the cadence of his words.

When I write about intimacy and emotional growth without a boyfriend, much of my inspiration comes from him.

"In my three books I've discovered I've been writing about only two themes," Choy tells me. "Firstly, I'm saying love has no rules, the second is, family are the ones who love you."

The sixty-six-year-old's life seems to be built around this mantra. He currently co-owns two houses, with two different families, one with his "city family" and one with his "country family." In both cases they are a straight couple with one or more kids, and Choy is their godfather. The houses aren't split up into apartments, they live together. When I pay him a visit at his "city home," I comment on the golf balls, clubs, and mini-put course in the living room.

"Are those yours?" I ask.

"Oh, please. Those are Karl's. Can you tell he's straight?"

People can't quite seem to wrap their head around the concept of this gay Asian man in his sixties cohabiting with this straight white family in a house that has not been subdivided. Now they just tell people he's a boarder, because that's as far as their limited comprehension is able to extend. But it is clear that the relationship is far more than that.

"There's a point in our belonging together, in our being together, that we became more belonging than being. I don't understand it, but I'm very moved by the fact that it happened."

It has manifested itself on countless occasions in Choy's life, including when his father became deathly ill. His father moved into the house and the whole family took care of him.

Like a great-grandfather, he held Karl and Marie's newborn daughter just months before he died.

"We have pictures of all that," Choy tells me wistfully.

It is an appropriate snapshot for a man who's been forced on several occasions to stare into the high beams of what it means to be family and to see what's beyond the blinding light.

In 2001 he suffered a severe asthma attack and had a near death experience. Without his extended family, he doesn't believe he would've survived. They rushed him to the emergency room in the middle of the night. His lungs were going into paralysis, and in order to get a tube past his gag reflex the doctors had to drug him up and induce a coma before he could be hooked up to a ventilator.

"When you're in that semi-coma you go in and out of it, and it's necessary to have people keep you alert to keep from going further into the darkness and not bothering coming back again, which can happen to people when they're heavily drugged. They can just surrender. So that was how my extended family proved themselves to be family. They were part of my recovery and called me back from a very dark place. And friends would do as much of course. The trick is, gay relationships often move into extended family situations, and rightly so because we have as much to offer as the family would."

Choy concludes, "Love has no rules, and unless one understands that we can't build a more humane community of one's own."

Not Quite There Just Yet

With Choy's words in mind I return to my own back-and-forth struggle for intimacy and growth outside of a boyfriend-style relationship. As Andrew Hostetler points out, "voluntary singlehood is not a *fait accompli*, and the choice to be single is not a discrete occurrence." In other words, this is not a developmental hump that maturing singles simply go through and then leave behind. "Rather, it is an ongoing project, a decision that needs to be renewed regularly (or retracted)," states Hostetler.

I think of one of these crises moments in my life, brought on by one of the worst sexual experiences I have ever had, which very much got me to questioning if single forever was a life I really wanted to lead. I felt very much alone, and far from the comforting company of men like Wayson Choy.

I went out with my friend Nate to a local Toronto dance club. Nate is the biggest crush I have ever had. We'd broken up as friends a few years before because I couldn't be around him anymore without feeling like shit because I had romantic feelings for him, which I knew he did not and never would return.

After a few years, our friendship has been able to resume, but there were growing pains, as I learned that night at the club we went to. I started chatting with these two guys, a pair of friends, who kept vying for my attention. They were both attractive, but to be honest, on their own I probably would not have been all that interested in either one. But watching them cock block each other as they outmaneuvered each other to talk with me over the course of the evening really stroked my ego. Having Nate there to see it all only added to the charge.

"What should I do?" I asked Nate at one point.

"Go for it" was his simple and drunken reply.

Going for it wound up including a snort of coke off the end of a key in a filthy bathroom stall, and then going home with one of the two dudes.

"Are you HIV negative?" he asked me once we were back at his place and half-naked.

"To the best of my knowledge." It was an honest reply.

"What does that mean, to the best of your knowledge?" he pressed.

"Well . . . I had unprotected sex less than three months ago, so it's too soon for me to get tested, but I was negative before that, so to the best of my knowledge, I don't have HIV."

Here I was talking about having had unprotected sex, something I was intentionally trying not to think about until it was time to get tested, and this guy that I wasn't really all that attracted to was looking at me like a potential disease, just as the social confidence of the coke was giving out from under me. I felt dirty. Not Christina Aguilera sex goddess dirty. More like scabby homeless guy dirty. Tainted. And for what? Because I wanted to be able to pick and choose between two paramours? Because I wanted to show off to Nate?

The evening culminated in us jerking off to a Matthew

Rush porn video. I nearly cheered when my "companion" came.

"Well, I don't think I'm going to be able to come . . ." I began, relieved to let my half-hard cock wilt.

"Oh, no, you're coming," he replied.

I suppose I could've walked out, but politeness seemed to demand that I oblige him. He tried stroking my legs and chest to help inspire me, but as I closed my eyes to go into my own fantasy world of muscle gods fucking I wanted to bat his touch away. It was too distracting.

After I finally came, I was left to wonder if this was "the more humane community of our own" that lay ahead for me without a boyfriend.

And so I began my journey to find sexual intimacy and further growth as a single gay man.

Fuck Buddies and Tricks *Are* Relationships

> *We all knew people who had their most magical experience very late one night at the Everard Baths with a man they never saw again, but of whose embraces they would think of periodically for the rest of their lives.*
>
> —Andrew Holleran, *Dancer from the Dance*

FLIP OPEN MY cell phone, dialing a number from memory. There's a click in my ear and a recorded message kicks in.

The number has been changed to . . .

I scribble down the new digits and redial. This time I get through. To voice mail.

"Josh, it's Steven."

I say what I have to say, hang up, and make a second call, this time from speed dial.

"Claude? Steven here. I need to book an emergency butt waxing."

If I'm going to do this, I've got to be ready.

Enter the fuck buddy.

The One Who Got Away

I've got it all worked out in my head. My voice mail to Josh is stage one in reestablishing contact with an old friend who, for three weeks, was the closest thing I had to a boyfriend. (As opposed to Vance. He was more like a husband.) We'd talk every few days, watch sci-fi together, buy each other silly little gifts (he knew my penchant for chocolate-covered almonds and indulged me with the good stuff—none of that cheap no-name nonsense), and naturally we'd have sex a couple of times a week. He'd sometimes even sneak off on his lunch hour and I'd meet him at his apartment for a quickie.

I'm not saying it was all I ever dreamed of, nor was it for him either. But he was smart, funny, athletic, liked to read, held my hand in public, and was a great kisser with a hot dancer's ass that would nestle my hard cock as we spooned through the night.

It all came to an end in the gayest way ever: during a trip to Ikea. As we approached the store from the parking lot I initiated the old, "so where is this going?" conversation.

By then we were at the sliding doors, crossing the Ikea threshold, and the answer to my question was left in the parking lot as we were enchanted by a world of randomly placed umlauts. After picking up a Grundtal shelf and appropriately enough a "Limbo" lamp, we began walking back toward the bus stop. As if a cosmic pause button had been released, we resumed the "where is this going?" conversation.

"I'm just trying to figure out what it is that we're doing. Are we just having sex, are we dating . . ."

I got no further before he cut in.

"Oh, we were *never* dating."

My surprise must have registered on my face, my eyes darting down to our transparent Ikea bags full of reasonably priced, pseudo-chic organizers. Was this not the very definition of gay dating? And how adamant he sounded, unable to get the words out fast enough to stamp out the blight that I'd suggested we might be engaged in.

He informed me of his hookups on a local sex line. I'm not sure why I was hurt. I knew he was having sex with other guys, not because we talked about it, but though a boy might lie to himself about such things, he's still aware. But there's knowing, and then there's *knowing*. It left me feeling somehow cheap.

It's been years since that day, but still, why call him now, after he hurt me like that?

As I have already proposed, I believe intimacy can come in different packages, ones that we don't honor because we've become so obsessed with the status of boyfriends and husbands.

I could've been getting some really nice company out of that fella over the years. It probably would've done a world of good for my self-growth. But I wasn't ready. Now I am. It's time to put theory into practice.

A day after my voice mail to Josh I check my inbox and there's an email from him.

> *Looking forward to seeing you! It's been too long. What's your sched these days?*
>
> *XOXO*
> *Josh*

My fingers are a flurry of keystrokes as I respond. In my voice mail I made no mention of sex. He's a horny guy, and he's made overtures since the Ikea incident, so I like to think of him as a sure thing, but safer to raise the ante one chip at a time to minimize the fallout in the event that he's not into a round of ride the pony.

> *Hey Josh. Can't wait to see you, too. Much to discuss. Did you know I've got a book contract? Anyway, you definitely need to come see my new condo. Still haven't had a chance to break it in :). I'm free in a couple of days. Let me know.*
>
> *XO*
> *S.*

I press send. A couple of days should be enough time for my cherry red ass to heal from the recent waxing, but still be silky smooth for our encounter. I can then wrap up this chapter on sex and the single gay guy.

I love it when everything can be so neatly scheduled.

In the meanwhile, I start checking out how the fuck buddy thing's working out for other gay men. After all, according to one study (Nardi and Sherrod) 76 percent of gay men surveyed said that they had engaged in sex with some of their close male friends, and 62 percent said they had sex with their casual male friends. Are they "suffering" from a lack of sexual intimacy, the kind that one can get in a relationship, assuming the couple's still having sex (with each other I mean), or are they onto something?

A Form of Intimacy Not to Be Sneezed At

During a one-day trip to Washington, D.C., I visit author Andrew Holleran. The lobby of his apartment building's an ode to art deco, but the unit he lives in is simple and sparse. In fact the walls are bare except for a Rembrandt Peale print of a man with tiny round spectacles next to a lush green geranium. Stacks of magazines, papers, and envelopes fill a table and a part of the surrounding floor.

The author himself gives off an aura like a spiritual tanning bed. His brown eyes sparkle, and his skin looks scrubbed fresher than a Jehovah's Witness going door to door. He's tall, with a lean, wiry frame and silver hair.

He's been writing about gay love for longer than I've been alive.

"If we were lucky and civilized we'd have one or two or three people we could have sex with over a long period of time," he tells me when I bring up the topic of sex and the single gay guy. "I think that's a form of intimacy not to be sneezed at. I'm going back to the fuck buddy, which sounds truly lustful, but I don't think it is. If you do have a fuck buddy you may know him for a long time, which inevitably introduces a form of intimacy."

I first became introduced to Holleran's writing years ago in the pages of *Dancer from the Dance*, which remains his most famous novel. I'd never done drugs or the party scene when I first read it. As a naif just out of the closet, I found the novel's flurry of experiences beyond my ken. Rereading it again for this book, I realized that the only part I remembered from the first time I read it was the scene in which the main character Malone returns to the apartment he shares with his boyfriend and finds that it's empty except for a mattress and his diary.

That moment was burned into mind.

It was so lonely. There are pitfalls to a sexual culture. But there are sex friends to be made.

Now that I'm a little more exposed and a little more worn, I realize that, like Larry Kramer's *Faggots*, *Dancer from the Dance* is the true *Sex and the City*, an A to Z guide for the gay romantic's search for love in the urban party scene. Of course not everyone's looking for love amid booze, loud music, and possibly drugs.

As Holleran points out, one can just go online now, referring me to the omnibus Web site craigslist.com, which people can use to post ads for places for rent, furniture for sale, and of course, love, love, love.

"I'm constantly looking at craigslist and it's basically a really pornographic meat market kind of place where people are reduced even more so than before the computer, to body parts, statistics, and it lays bare the poverty of the imagination. Everyone seems to be looking for a bisexual or straight military masculine athletic person with an eight-inch dick, and that's the template. . . . The bathhouse is actually more humane because you have to deal with the person in real time and converse even a little bit."

Which matches up with the motto imparted to him not long after he came out.

"The thing I was told very early on in my gay life was that it's not enough to go to bed with someone. You have to talk with them afterward, and I thought absolutely not, I don't care if I talk with them afterward, I just want to go to bed with them. I thought that was absolutely trying to mix something that you shouldn't mix, and was a rather sentimental thing. Now, after many, many years, that's all that matters to me almost."

In other words, he doesn't present the fuck buddy option lightly, nor does it come from a fuck-the-system political manifesto. It's derived from his own experience, and from what he's observed over several decades of gay life as something that can work as both sexual *and* intimate.

So how did Holleran reach this current stance?

Getting Over the Hump

He's never done the live-together-for-years thing, but he has had lovers who he would consider "great loves." He hasn't seriously dated anyone since publishing his novel *Nights in Aruba*, about twenty years ago, and the last time he had a "terrible" emotional attachment was more than a decade ago, while living in a small town in Florida.

"I thought this is just too perfect. I've found someone I'm actually in love with. He lived in this town, too, and that's it. Everything is here. I can have my small town life *and* I can have the rest."

He wrote about the experience in his 1996 novel *The Beauty of Men*. Like *Dancer from the Dance* it is a love story, but one that could not be further from the frenetic sexuality of New York in the '70s. It focuses instead on the character of Lark, who like Holleran, was living in a small Florida town, looking after his paralyzed mother, the pair of them watching episodes of *Murder She Wrote* when Lark's not off looking for anonymous hookups at drive-in cruising spots.

During one such scene, Lark's friend Ernie counsels with a laugh, "I certainly don't come here to fall in love. . . . And if you do, that's because you're still in transition!" Ernie not only mocks Lark but also the younger men to whom he's invisible.

He doesn't even bother with the baths because he does better with his shirt on and only his mouth to offer.

"On paper, Ernie is the nightmare of homosexuals—living by himself in a small town with his cats and dogs—but in fact he seems content."

Lark, on the other hand, is desperately pining over, basically stalking a man in his thirties who wants nothing to do with him. Ernie may be the nightmare of homosexuals, but I prefer him to Lark as an example of how to be gay and single. And while the character of Lark hasn't transitioned, Holleran certainly has, based on his own life narrative that he fictionalizes with painful honesty and longing in *The Beauty of Men*.

Twelve years later, he tells me, "After that [guy], nothing. And growing older, getting more independent, more attached to my own habits and the solitary life, I grew to get over that hump."

It is a crucible he believes many of us go through. On the other side he has come to recognize a bevy of alternative intimacies. His writing is full of them, from being in love with the best friend/roommate (hello *Queer as Folk* and *Will & Grace*) to the mother/gay son bond.

"Lark is constantly going to the boat ramp and falls in love with a guy who drives him crazy and at the same time he's having an intimate life bound up with his caretaking," says Holleran. "The thing with Becker doesn't pan out, and the rich emotional bond was mummy-kins. Life is what happens when you're busy doing something else."

Now in his late fifties (he'll be no more specific), Holleran muses, "the irony is the person I've had sex with the longest is someone I don't consider a boyfriend, and who I sleep with every three or four months, and it's outside all the pressures of being a boyfriend."

He emphasizes once again that this fuck buddy scenario does introduce a form of intimacy. Not only that, but there are consequences to gay men who try to ignore this reality, adopting a form of denial that leaves them ill equipped to deal with the emotions that come with the territory.

Honor Thy Tricks

In other words, just because gay men *think* they've separated sex and emotion does not mean they've actually done so, a scenario that Michael Shernoff has seen playing out in his patients.

Shernoff's been a psychotherapist since 1975, and in addition to his private practice in Manhattan, he has authored and edited several books on mental health issues for gay men and HIV, and is on the faculty at Columbia University School of Social Work. He has also written for *In the Family*, a magazine that focuses on queer relationships, In "Unexamined Loss: An Expanded View of Gay Break-Ups," Shernoff looks beyond traditionally recognized emotional liaisons.

"While gay men, reflecting the larger culture's biases and prejudices, don't acknowledge break-ups apart from traditional-looking committed relationships, many of them end up in therapy complaining about feeling mysteriously depressed, frustrated, and confused about their lives. Often, I have to gently push to get them to admit that they are allowed to feel sorrow and loss over an unconventional break-up," writes Shernoff.

He's specifically referring to affairs and casual sex partners.

And while some may feel that these sorts of "relationships" are too casual to qualify as breakups when they end, Shernoff maintains that such an attitude serves only to reinforce the stereotype that gay men are "sexual machines." Instead he encourages us to recognize that these encounters touch us on a variety of levels, and he pushes his clients to empathize with the men they engage with, rather than reduce them or oneself to an object.

As Andrew Sullivan writes in *Love Undetectable*, "The meeting of two human beings in a sexual encounter can never be a neutral or a casual phenomenon. It has meaning, and danger, and promise." After all, there are many reasons to have sex; horniness, loneliness, happiness, unhappiness. Desire is more than a hard-on.

In the so-called sex-mad '70s the author of *Gay Macho: The Life and Death of the Homosexual Clone*, notes of the sexual "clone" culture of the time that tricking can involve "tenderness, affection and companionship."

Even in one of the most anonymous types of gay encounters, in public restrooms, otherwise known as tearooms, there's an unconventional sentimentality. Though words are rarely exchanged, "participants may develop strong attachments to the settings of their adventures in impersonal sex," writes Laud Humphreys in his groundbreaking sociological study, *Tearoom Trade: Impersonal Sex in Public Spaces*. "I have noted more than once that these men seem to acquire stronger sentimental attachments to the buildings in which they meet for sex than to the persons with whom they engage in it." Humphreys notes one gay man laid down a wreath at the site of a tearoom after it had been demolished. Fuck buddies could learn from this example.

"Many gay men don't allow themselves to mourn the loss of their various relationships, including affairs and casual sexual partners, relationships that may have had vague emotional parameters yet were still meaningful in their lives because they had come to mean companionship, warmth, romance, homosocial contact and pleasure," insists Shernoff.

This applies not only to singles of course. With nonmonogamous gay couples there's the added factor of jealousy. Should one partner lose a fuck buddy, he's not likely to be allowed to show a sense of loss in front of the remaining boyfriend, who might take it as a sign of emotional infidelity. It is another level of pretending that a fuck buddy is not a relationship.

But for myself I wonder more about how I as a single gay man can allow more trust, honesty, and intimacy into my own casual encounters, including the fuck buddy scenario.

Back to Fuck Buddy Josh

I think of Josh, and the Ikea incident. Despite him saying "we were never dating" we remained friends, bound by some common social ties, and many common interests. The real clincher for me, though, was one evening, as I literally found myself on the verge of an emotional breakdown. I'd just started a new job, which meant that I was now working two part-time jobs, which I discovered was way worse than one full-time job. I was also trying to fix up my apartment to rent out while at the same time sprucing up my basement apartment to move into, while at the same time already moving stuff down there.

It was the painting that finally did me in.

Whatever twisted god gave gay men the gift of color, he or she obviously passed me by, for I have no sense of it. I picked a green which was OK, and another color that can only be described as lavender, though that's not what it looked like to me on the paint swatch. After rolling it onto one wall, I stared at it in dismay and ran off to the paint store with the can of paint to see if they could tone it down.

I came back and did another coat. Now it was neon.

It was late. I was tired, I was overwhelmed. In that moment I, who have maintained steady control of my emotions since I was a teenager, felt myself unravel inside. Is this what other people went through on a regular basis? No wonder they were all so uselessly dependent!

And yet I knew I'd surpassed my limits.

There was this foreign cracking along interior fault lines I didn't even know were there. I never understood the phrase falling to pieces until I realized that's exactly what I was feeling about to happen.

The phone rang and on the other end was Josh.

I broke down and told him everything, not quite crying, but the speed and pitch of my voice betraying it all.

"You know, I could come over and help," he offered immediately.

Normally I would say no, for to accept help would be to be in someone's debt, and who knew when they'd come to collect. But I was destitute.

"Really?" I must have sounded beyond pathetic, and when he arrived on his bike ten minutes later, he laughed at the paint colors, and I smiled sheepishly and he gave me a big hug and helped me find a better color and apply it.

Since then I've helped him move twice, just as he helped me finish moving my stuff into that apartment once the painting was done. And when it comes to our past sexual liaisons, perhaps I was too quick to throw the bathwater out with the baby. I am now encouraged and inspired to give it another go, in part by those who have a handle on their own fuck buddy situation, in part by acknowledging the intimacy and commitment that exists even in what is ostensibly *perceived* as a casual scenario but which can still draw layers of trust and commitment into play, as I learn from a true fuck buddy aficionado.

Long-Term Fuck Buddies

The fuck buddy relationship is one that's worked so well for Brad Fraser that most of his relationships over the past ten years have been very intimate fuck buddies. The forty-five-year-old is the playwright behind such works as *Poor Superman* and *Love and Human Remains*, the director of the movie *Leaving Metropolis*, former talk show host on Canada's gay TV network PrideVision and writer and coproducer for three seasons on the hit American TV series *Queer as Folk*.

"Everyone's become obsessed with a relationship that could lead to marriage," says Fraser. "Relationships are not something you shop for. They're out of your control. To be out looking for a relationship is the biggest way to not have one, and I see a lot of gays going out trying to create relationships that lead to marriage."

He tells me this as he takes a break from sorting through three thousand comic books that he'd thought lost in storage years ago but which have suddenly turned up again and were delivered to his home the day before. What to keep and what to throw away? Sounds like a game of emotional poker. But aside from his penchant for men in tights, he has plenty to say about keepers.

"One of these intimate fuck buddies I have seen a minimum of two times per week for eight years, and we have a very intimate relationship," he tells me. "We'll go out and do things, and I do consider it a long-term relationship but not as a spouse or lover."

The forty-five-year-old has given that whole bit a try though, back in his twenties and thirties. That's when he was into serial relationships and believed they were meant to last forever. Now he doesn't hold to such pretensions.

"The last long-term relationship I had was in my early thirties. We lived together for five years and that was when I
decided everything we are told about relationships was fiction."

Interestingly it's not that he doesn't believe in love or even
falling in love, he just doesn't want to share his space and life
24/7. During another attempt at an LTR he realized that
falling asleep together and waking up together every morning
was a nightmare.

And he doesn't see couples possessing anything he doesn't.
Sexually speaking, a couple of studies indicate that single gays
and gays in couples are equally satisfied with their sex lives.
And while Fraser supports gay marriage (everyone has the
same right to fuck things up, he tells me), his current view is
that most of the long-term relationships he knows are "so dysfunctional just through repetition, the idea appalls me.

"I don't feel like they're any closer to where they want to be
in their life than I am, or any less lonely. . . . And I feel the
relationship has become an excuse not to progress as a
person."

All the same, in a bundle of seeming contradictions he
asserts, "This does not mean that I don't believe in marriage,
or that two people can't make it work. The two correct per-
sonalities can absolutely work together, and could work for
me in the future"—if, for instance, he weren't constantly traveling because of work, or if he "met the right person who
makes me want to spend every second of every day of my life
together."

And Fraser insists that when he *is* in a relationship, he's a good boyfriend.

"There are some of those gay guys who say shut up and suck my cock, and I'm only occasionally like that. . . . I like having that other person to listen to and confide in . . . but not when I'm working."

As the interview with Fraser winds down, I'm full of bubbles as I plan to get back in the fuck buddy game.

Snake Eyes

I check my email, and sure enough Josh's written back.

Hey! Listen, Sunday won't work after all. We HAVE to catch up, including why Sunday won't work. Hehehehe :) cheers!

That two-timing double-crossing whore.

OK, so maybe I'm a little emotional when it comes to rejection. And maybe I overplayed my hand in assuming that I could simply snap my fingers and resume where things left off with Josh. I should probably add that Josh and I *have* done the nasty since the Ikea incident (New Year's and champagne can have an effect on a fella), and he *has* offered to do it again. All the same, it's been a while, and he's not one to collect dust. I guess I was just too slow on the uptake, and now I'm left licking my wounded pride.

But I supposed that just proves the point. These are not emotionless affairs, at least not for me. That presents the challenge of how to keep an open heart, when the inclination is to close it from fear of getting hurt.

I think back to something Andrew Holleran said to me.

"Gay people go through a lot of battering. When you think of a straight man and his emotional and sexual history, and women, how many times do you think a straight man or straight woman will fall in love over the course of their lives? Once for some, twice for others, four or five is a lot for a straight person.

"But for the gay person, their little hearts are constantly opening, ready to make this attachment. Having it not work out, the scar tissue builds up. I just think they're battered. Not battered spouses, but battered lovers. That's where so much of gay humor comes from. You have to grow a thick skin about it to the point where a lot of our language sounds like prostitutes talking. We sound like girls who've been around the block and who've had a lot of clients and we're kind of tough in a worldly wise way, but the sad part about it is that most people I don't think are expected to go through that unless you are a prostitute, and why should we have to?"

His words really get me to thinking about the potential downside of a relationship that's not etched in stone. And yet I am stubborn. I've read a *lot* of gay relationship books as part of my research, and I'm still convinced that fuck buddies and even one-night stands *are* a relationship, potentially good ones, even if often short-lived. One of the things all the relationship books written by therapists emphasize is communication—open, honest, and not defensive. If these unconventional sexual liaisons are relationships, then the benefits of communication should also hold true in these scenarios.

With this in mind, I reissue my invitation to Josh.

The Talk, *Again*

"I hope you're not going to hate me for this," I say to Josh as he sits on my couch sipping his tea.

He sets the mug down.

"Why would I hate you?" he asks.

Because you hurt me, I want to tell him. *Because I wrote about it. Because I don't think you're going to like what I have to say. Because if you start getting defensive I probably will, too.*

I can't get the words out, and simply hand him an early draft of the chapter on fuck buddies.

"So I'm supposed to read the stuff you've written about me and then correct everything that you got wrong?" he asks.

"Pretty much."

I keep my tone light and breezy even as my stomach clenches and I feel a bout of anxiety-driven nausea. I turn to tidy the kitchen because I have to keep myself busy or I'll go crazy while he reads. As I load the dishwasher, he flips through the pages and barks out a laugh or two.

At one point, I hear a deep and long sigh.

I pour soap crystals into the dishwasher and turn it on as Josh finishes reading.

"I love that you mention the painting," he tells me, the pages curled in his hand like a scroll. He's referring to my botched attempts at adding some color to the walls of my last apartment. "I don't think you really describe how bad the colors were though, like plastic alligator green and Malibu Barbie pink."

"I swear to god that's not what they looked like on the swatches."

"You tried so determinedly to fix it."

I nod and avert my eyes, both of us knowing we're not here to discuss paint palettes. We're here to talk about Ikea, about his snap answer that "we were never dating."

"My intention had been to be honest," he explains. "I thought, I have to fix this right away, and it was reactionary. I'd been more abrupt than I'd meant to be. I'd been cruel, and that was not my intention. But I'm pretty sure I called you and said I didn't mean to be that harsh."

"I don't remember that," I reply. "But you may have. I believe you, I just don't remember it."

I'm convinced he never called, but who can say? It was a long time ago. I can't believe we're even talking about this now.

"I'm surprised that I would've responded so harshly to the word dating," he adds.

"I felt like I'd pressed some sort of panic button."

"Probably. You met me in my first season at a new dance company. There had been several months of fear that I'd never dance again because of an injury. Now my dance career was coming back, and I'd just moved to Toronto from Calgary. I wanted to be in the big city."

"You wanted to play."

"You want to play, you want to be you, and not be a part of something with someone else. It's certainly not that I wasn't attracted to you, or that there weren't those possibilities, it just wasn't where I was at."

He hands the chapter back to me. I click open a three-ring binder and slide the punctured sheets into place, figuring that's all we have to talk about, that I've got all I need, and I can turn off the tape recorder. But of course that would be too easy.

"I'm totally fine with everything in here," Josh says. "I have no issues at all with what you've written. But something you should know. When we met, you portrayed yourself very confidently, all the time, and you can admit now that you weren't that experienced or confident when I met you, but that's definitely not how you portray yourself, and I have a feeling I didn't realize what was portrayal and what was you until I opened my big mouth."

It's weird hearing this, and watching him muse back to those early first encounters.

"You were pretty casual. Easygoing. There definitely wasn't a sense of emotional vulnerability. You were tall, classically handsome, all in black, confident. And that was a characteristic of you at the time, of putting on a very strong confident outer look."

Some things haven't changed, and yet they must, if I am to grow in or outside of a relationship. I guess that's why I've asked him here. To let what's on the inside out, and to just listen to his story. It also turns into a chance to remember that whatever hurts may have come from our tryst, I got a lot out of it that I would not dream of trading in.

There was the physical intimacy of course. It took a lot of patience on his part, and a lot of trust on mine, but I finally relaxed enough for him to get the dildo Magnum up my ass. It's only years and many experiences later that I now realize how nice it is to be with a guy who's caring and attentive enough to go at such a gracious pace. But there is more.

"Obviously there's a lot between us," says Josh. "We've remained friends, and we communicate quite well, but at that point I was just thinking, wow, I can make him take this big blue thing up his butt."

"Actually it was green."

"Blue," he insists.

I go to the bedroom to pull it out.

"I might be willing to go as far as aqua," he shouts from the living room.

As I dust it off (it's been a while), I reflect on the nonphysical intimacy we've shared, like when he came to a couple of my tattoo appointments. I sat in a massage chair, my forehead, chin, and chest pressed into a padded chair as the artist's needle jabbed in and out of my back. Josh held my hand and fed me chocolate-covered almonds to keep my sugar levels up during the exhausting process.

More than twenty hours spread over five appointments later, and the tattoo was done, camouflaging the scars from the cystic acne of my teenage years. The scars are still there. They will *always* be there. That is the nature of scars, physical or emotional. They are a part of who I am. They tell a part of my story. But so, too, does the tattoo. It's part of *my* narrative solution. Where before I only saw ugliness, I now see beauty. Twin serpents coil up from the base of my spine, their heads flaring out over my shoulder blades, all done in a Middle Eastern style as opposed to biker-chic. It's a caduceus, the staff carried by the messenger Hermes, and a symbol of healing.

Even years later, Josh is more excited to tell people about my tattoos than I am. I smile at this as I emerge from the bedroom, nine-inch Magnum in hand.

"It's not as big as I remember," says Josh.

"It never is."

We agree that it is the color teal.

Boyfriends Can Be Like Prostitutes— Prostitutes Can Be Like Boyfriends

When you live together sex takes on a whole new dimension. I feel like a prostitute that works for really low rates. I'll do oral and anal, if you take out the garbage. I'll lick your balls, if you open this jar. Do I have to eat your ass to get you to mow the lawn?

—Margaret Cho, *Revolution*

I AM EXTREMELY CHEAP.

When I was a little kid, my mom gave me and my brothers a quarter apiece so that each of us could buy a super bouncy rubber ball. My brothers ran off immediately to slide their twenty-five-cent piece into what looked like a gumball machine and collect their multicolored prize. But I hesitated.

They're going to lose their super bouncy rubber balls in about five minutes, I thought to myself.

My quarter went into the bank. A few moments of super bouncy rubber fun followed by the inevitable emotional crash when the ball bounced too fast for the eye to follow and disappeared seemingly into nowhere could not compare with the thrill of compound interest.

So when I suggest paying for sex as a long-term option for erotic and sexual fulfillment, I do not do so lightly. But if I am to honestly explore long-term sexual intimacy outside a boyfriend relationship, I am obliged to at least propose it, as this is an option that some men are pursuing, and there's even an advocate for such an arrangement, as embodied by Joseph Itiel's book *Sex Workers as Virtual Boyfriends*.

"Regular 'regulars' are good candidates for becoming virtual boyfriends," he writes. "Michael and I recently reached a milestone—our three hundredth sex session. This could not have happened without a genuine liking for each other," he writes.

"By being willing to talk," he insists, "I have learned a lot from my sex workers, probably more than from my free sexual encounters. Men I meet socially often converse about subjects with which I have some familiarity, such as current events, movies, the stock market, and literature. My sex workers, especially the ones I have picked up on the streets, have taught me things which ordinarily I would never have learned."

I have to be honest that I'm not 100 percent comfortable contemplating this as an option for myself, but nor can I simply ignore it when considering what my choices will be as I get older and find it more difficult to attract the kinds of guys who turn me on. God knows it's hard enough to lure them in as it is.

Doris Day once sang *que sera, sera* . . . but if I am to be single forever, I'm going to have to at least consider options that are not on the top of my list. That could mean paying for sex, or perhaps giving it up.

Giving Up Sex Is Not the End of the World

I think back to a sunny winter's day about a year ago when I was working on the article on which this book is based. I met with a veteran of this so-called gay love life, the pair of us huddled together under the buzz of the fluorescent lights of the Pizza Pizza at Church and Wellesley streets, the nexus of Toronto's gay village. We wound up at this "glamorous" locale because the café at the local community center was closed, and as he'd had both knees replaced three years prior, we decided not to venture far on snowy sidewalks.

"The surgery made me older," he confided. "I've aged a lot."

His name is Alan Raeburn, his soft British accent perfect for the theater critic career he successfully pursued for many years but discordant with the greasy cheese on my pizza slice. He grew up in Liverpool, England, and at sixteen his family moved to Kitchener, Ontario. Two years later he was bound for Toronto to study Radio and TV Arts at Ryerson, the same school where Eric McCormack would one day train before going on to star as Will Truman in *Will & Grace*.

But the concept of a weekly series starring a fag and his hag five decades later was not even a blip on the radar of eighteen-year-old Alan Raeburn.

The year was 1954.

"I'd just been fucked for the first time by a community theater director. He broke me in." Raeburn winks.

Now in his late sixties, he remembers the days when dancing meant a quiet fox-trot. "A rising erection indicated if you'd go any further," he mused, taking a sip from his can of ginger ale.

Over his life he's had several serious relationships, including five years with Louise, a woman he'd met when living in New York. It was, in part, a response to being dumped by the love of his life, who was supposed to move back with Alan to Toronto. The boyfriend of three years bailed at the last minute to stay with his New York circle of friends.

Alan was thirty-two at the time.

"Jimmy broke my heart," he said, eyes shimmering ever so slightly behind his bifocals. "He was a southern boy, blond, blue eyed, and bushy tailed. Skinny except for one place, and that made up for the skinny."

He smiled impishly before his tone turned wistful.

"He cared for me."

Thirty-six years later he said: "I don't boo hoo over it, but there's a sense of loneliness. I have friends to do things with but it would be nice to have someone in my life."

But when it comes to dating now, he said he doesn't go to

bars (they make him feel like an "old codger"), and he thinks his waist size is too big for the baths.

"There was a time when you're younger when you have to go out because you don't know what you might be missing," he said. "You go to see if Mr. Perfect's going to be out there."

There's no hint of bitterness, though. He was young once, "I had that," he explained, and when he looks at younger gay men he knows "they're going to get old, too, one day." He's now involved with Toronto's Older GLBT club at the queer-geared 519 Community Centre, and another group called Prime Timers. He's met men of his age that he's attracted to but hasn't felt a "reciprocation."

"What about hustlers?" I asked hesitantly, not sure if it's an insult to present this as an option.

"Oh no!" he chuckled good-naturedly. "I can't afford them. But I would if I could."

Besides, he says his sex drive's not what it used to be. Still, it's nice to know that paying for sex is up for discussion. But for those who really want to consider this option, the person to talk with is Hungry Helga, so-called because of his appetite for sex on the meter.

Hookers and Nothing But

Hungry Helga's retired, and he's made a point of making love for hire a significant part of his pension budget. Also, he's a singles purist, a lifer if you will, who's never had a relationship and genuinely doesn't seem to want one.

"I think everyone gets lonely once in a while," he says with a Buddha-like nonchalance. "It's a normal thing, but this is the way I choose to live."

When Helga turned sixty-three, a few days prior to the big day, he confessed to me in his deep, New York accent, he was hoping one of his little "social workers" was going to give him a freebie as a present.

"He did at Christmas," he says. "That was a shock."

Helga's first time with a guy was at age thirty-seven. The fellow was a hustler, and Helga hasn't looked back. As for relationships? "I think I may have thought about it once or twice, but I know people who've had relationships. They break up and they go to pieces, and the person you love, now you hate them. I couldn't put myself through that. I couldn't handle the breakup."

But along the way he has forged some unusual friendships, as may be expected from someone who picked up his first hustler twenty-six years ago, and who did up to seven tricks a day at his peak. "I've known some of them for ten to twelve years," he says. "They're not kids, they're getting old."

In one case, he's using air miles to fly down a Toronto escort. "We'll go to Universal Studios, but there's no payment [or sex] involved. It's just a social visit."

In *Sex Workers as Virtual Boyfriends* these are among the scenarios that Joseph Itiel describes happening to himself, where a "sex-plus" relationship can grow into an "abiding nonsexual friendship."

Sex-Plus and Money-Plus

What Itiel means by a sex-plus relationship would be one in which the client is getting something above and beyond sex, be it a common social activity, an intellectual pursuit, or a spiritual practice. For the sex worker this is a "money-plus" situation, where he's getting a payoff above and beyond his fee because on some level he enjoys his john's company, and perhaps he even gets something of a mentor out of the situation. For his part Itiel has learned about a slew of things he'd never have otherwise explored, from hip hop to wicca, and one of his former boys for hire later became his computer expert.

"Because of the physical and sometimes emotional intimacy with sex workers, there can be more than a sex-for-money transaction," he says, though he warns this will certainly not always be the situation. It probably won't even be the majority of cases. And he strongly cautions against trying to pay someone to be your actual lover, which he says is almost certainly doomed to failure.

He calls this a de facto sugar daddy relationship.

"As a rule in such relationships, the 'son' thinks that his 'daddy' does not bestow sufficient 'sugar' on him. The daddy feels shortchanged because, invariably, the son does not give him enough sex and, to boot, doesn't show true filial gratitude."

In other words, there is a difference between virtual and literal boyfriends, and Itiel insists it's key to keep this in mind when negotiating this nebulous territory.

And of course there are more obvious risks, like getting conned, assaulted, or robbed. Though with the number of times gay men let strangers into their homes, it's a miracle how infrequently this seems to take place.

Still, for safety reasons Helga generally relies on referrals from friends or hustlers he knows and trusts rather than picking just anyone up off the street. Escorts are much more expensive (because of the overhead of a Web site, cell phone, pager, as well as their higher level of looks and professionalism, he explains), so as a frugality he reserves those for special occasions or when he's traveling.

"It can be an expense," he admits, but his condo's paid for, so beyond maintenance fees, utility bills, and food, he's got money to spare from his retirement funds.

As a freelance writer, with no pension (or boyfriend) in sight, I'm left wondering if I should start putting money away into hustler RRSPs, alongside my plastic surgery savings account.

Some might view this as insulting to older gays, not to mention a reflection of my own vanity and fears of aging (which is totally bang on, single or otherwise), but according to Dick Moore, the Coordinator for the 519's Older GLBT group, the things older gay singles need to think about are "health, money, positive attitude . . . and a close network of chosen family." And I would argue that if a group of friends is my emotional retirement fund, then my sexual well-being needs an equivalent backup plan.

Helga seems to be happy and sexually satisfied. When I

reach that age I intend to be as well. But for all my bluster and sex-positivism, am I really comfortable *paying* for it? Is that why I've reduced my diet to brown rice, chicken breasts, salmon, and cans of tuna? I'm not sure why this should be a big deal for me. I was practically addicted to lap dances soon after I moved to Toronto.

My obsession with peelers eventually ran its course. The thrill of finally being allowed to touch those kinds of muscled bodies diminished, though it has never fully disappeared. So the question is, do I really want to return to that type of route, except with an orgasm now tacked on at the end? Is that a future I want to be open to?

Only one way to find out.

My First Time

My heart is racing as I visit a massage parlor not far from where I live. I'd expected the boys to be lounging around in the lobby so I could snap my fingers at the one I wanted. The chairs are empty in the dimly lit area, and I have to wait a few moments before the receptionist comes to the front. He's in his early twenties, cute in an average sort of way.

Trying my best not to appear as nervous as I feel, I try to get the scoop on the situation.

"So are these *full* body massages?" I ask.

"Oh, yes," he assures me, although there's no wink wink in his tone, so I'm not at all sure if we're talking about the same thing. "What kind of guy are you looking for?"

"Muscular, smooth, youngish," I reply.

"Hmmm . . . that could be tough. We have muscular, and we have smooth, but the two together . . ."

With an effort I keep my eyes from rolling. Since when is muscular *and* smooth such an unrealistic request? Body fascism just isn't what it used to be. And as Itiel points out, "maddeningly, all too often the more *un*attractive the masseur the more professional his massage, and vice versa."

The receptionist flips through his schedule book.

"Come back tomorrow," he tells me. "There is someone scheduled who's muscular and smooth. Ask for Nexxus."

I nod in a noncommittal fashion. At home, I try going online and quickly discover the nightmare of the virtual hunt. Most of the escorts' pics are hideous.

You should be paying me, I think to myself.

I call Hungry Helga, thinking that perhaps a guided tour of Florida's sex-for-sale scene might be the way to go. It's been a while since we last spoke, and unfortunately since then all of his "little friends" have been arrested on a variety of offenses, including theft and breaking parole.

God damn it, what does it take to hire a decent whore these days? Frankly, this is more work than picking up at a bar.

"That's because you've never done this before," a friend of mine explains. And it's true. I used to be equally useless at cruising. Eye contact. It's all in the eye contact.

And now here I am, equally timid, equally unsure of the emotional ramifications of what I'm about to embark on. And so I ignore the stigma attached to sex for sale and listen to what advice my friend has to offer.

He recommends I try the massage parlor I already visited today. He laughs when I tell him it wasn't clear if the massages were sexual.

"Darling, when the door closes, that's when you start to negotiate. What you pay to the front desk is *just* for the room."

And sure enough, a day later I'm naked on the table paying an extra $80.00 for "Nexxus" to get naked himself, give me a hand job, and to let me touch him.

"Just be careful with my dick. It's kind of chaffed from jerking off at my Web cam job," he cautions.

I assure him that I have no interest in his dick, which doesn't seem to make him feel better. After stripping down, he briefly goes through the motions of massaging my calf, but that degenerates into a conversation about our respective tattoos, and how he used to want to be a tattoo artist, which segues into his sob story of a slutty mother who didn't love him and how he'd like to have a mentor.

"Hey, do you think five thousand dollars is a lot of money to have saved up?" he asks.

"Uh . . . that depends. How much money do you want to have saved?"

"About a hundred grand."

"And what would you do if you did have that much money?"

"I'd buy a sports car. Get some electrolysis done. New clothes. Weed."

I redirect his hands to my legs and start stroking his smooth forearms.

He stops for a moment, rubbing *Purell* antibacterial hand sanitizer between his palms, to neutralize the massage oil he explains, before slipping on latex finger condoms.

"Cum can get stuck under the fingernails for *weeks*," he warns me as he rolls latex over his digits.

As he starts playing with my cock, I drag him in close, hugging his hard body tight against me, relishing his free arm slipping under my back and squeezing me into him. I start getting hard and my lips find their way to his neck, pecking him gently. After the fourth kiss he pulls away just a little too quickly.

"So you better come soon, 'cause your session's almost over," he half-whispers in a throaty kind of way.

I glance at the clock. I actually have twenty minutes left, but we are agreed in our desire for this to end sooner rather than later. Without kissing I just don't see myself getting into this, so I run a porn loop in my mind, as I always do when duty calls for a come shot even though the specific guy and/or circumstances haven't a hope in hell of stimulating one. But for eighty bucks, I'm not leaving without squirting.

And there we go.

Wipe, dress, pay, home.

As I regale this tale at a gay dinner party of enthusiastic listeners later that week, I am consoled by the man sitting across from me as a plate of steaming lasagna is placed before him. After four years of ups and downs, he recently ended his relationship. But during their time together, it was he who covered most of the bills for both of them, including their trips to Miami.

"I paid for *my* whore for four years," he says of his ex-boyfriend, who was underemployed and overly financially dependant on him. "And I didn't get that great of a massage or hand job either. I got mostly half-assed blow jobs that petered out halfway through. He got off a lot, though. Not that I'm bitter. His sister said to me that I could get a real prostitute, a really good one for the amount of money I spent on him. And that's his sister."

We all raise our glasses to that.

It's good to know that despite societal pretensions, boyfriends can often be in an unspoken arrangement involving as much barter as love. So while I may be far from mastering a "virtual boyfriend" arrangement, there are those who have. Some are just more honest about it than others. And as I wade through these foreign waters, I do make progress, and ultimately discover that not all whores are created equally.

Sexological Body Workers

"I would guess that half my clients are men in some form of relationship, from straight to bi to gay, and they're not getting what they need," says sexological body worker Paul Barber.

Basically, he's a *highly* trained sex worker, though there are certain services he does not provide, like fucking. And he couldn't be more different than smooth and muscled Nexxus. Barber's clearly got strong arms but also something of a belly, and his goatee is white as can be. But there is a spark in his eye, and the sureness in his voice is matched by the skill of his touch.

Some come to him individually for new experiences, others want to improve their prowess for their partner. In such instances he's taking on the role of sexual surrogate and mentor. Again, this is a role I once assumed a boyfriend must fill.

The other half of his clients "are people who want to explore their sexuality, their eroticism, or they just need touch. This comes down to what's missing when you're not in a relationship, significant touch. Something that has a little more weight to it than a hug from your mom and dad, something you can't get from your work colleagues. . . . They need to be touched. It sustains them to deal with their life."

Among this group he includes a group of six clients, aged twenty-five to thirty-five, whom he refers to as his "young tribe." Some he says are of porn star caliber. "They've got the looks, but because they don't have the self-esteem they can be taken advantage of, so I'm a butch mother to those guys."

Barber's credentials include the Body Electric's Sacred Intimate Course and years of official fieldwork. Founded in 1984, the Body Electric School helps people get more in touch with their bodies through various breathing, stretching, and massage exercises. The Sacred Intimate training takes these skills for healing through eroticism to a much higher level and is inspired by the idea of "sacred" or temple whores.

"Sacred intimacy is holding a mirror up to people and allowing them to fall in love with themselves," says the school's director, Collin Brown, in an interview for *White Crane: Journal for the Exploration of Gay Men's Spirituality.* "This was the role of the sacred prostitutes in the temples, to mirror the divinity and let people see the god inside of themselves. There is this wonderful story of sacred prostitutes being with men who came back from war. Their job was to love the warriors so they could come back into the society and not be filled with war."

After all of the childhood crap and homo trauma, I'm ready to leave the dating battlefield behind.

"In my practice a lot of gay men are not engaged with their body," says Barber. "They're totally disengaged, like the gearshift is in neutral."

And if you can't feel your body, you can't feel your emotions, if you can't feel your emotions you can't be in the moment, or express what's going on inside of you, or revel in who you really are. You can't be intimate. You can't be yourself. So can a sex worker like Barber take on the role of substitute boyfriend, at least to a degree? At the very least he can help his clients feel more connected to other people, which is what many people are seeking from a relationship.

"My practice is about getting the client out of his head and into his body, to really feel his core," Barber tells me as I lie down on his massage table. "And when we're connected with our bodies we're in a better state to connect with other men."

He massages me lightly for about fifteen minutes, then the pressure builds in intensity.

"I would encourage you to start moving your body," he tells me.

My hips gyrate into and out of his strokes.

"You have a very expressive cock," he says as he plays with my hard-on. No mental porn loop required. "I imagine you'd be a very good top."

I reach over my head to grip the end of the massage table for extra support. Comparing this to the crappy rub and tug I tried months before, I realize not all hand jobs are created equal.

"Becoming embodied, feeling your body, is to know yourself," he says. "The next thing is to speak it."

He clasps my balls, rubbing them with hot oil, and rakes his fingernails over my scrotum, making me gurgle.

"You like that?" he asks.

"Oh, yeah."

"Do you think you'd be able to ask a guy to do that for you?"

You bet. But this is not simply about honesty in sexual touch.

"You can only be intimate to the degree that you can be vulnerable," writes Dean Ornish, M.D., in *Love and Survival: The Scientific Basis for the Healing Power of Intimacy.* "You can only be vulnerable and open your heart to the degree that you feel safe—because if you make yourself vulnerable, you might get hurt. Commitment creates safety and makes intimacy possible."

Ornish is best known for devising a low-fat diet for preventing and reversing heart disease in books like *Eat More, Weigh Less.* Since so many of us eat our feelings by substituting food for love, perhaps it's appropriate that he writes not only about a diet that can heal the physiological heart. In his lesser-known work *Love & Survival* he delves into the healing power of human connections.

He says that lack of commitment results from fear, which leads to cynicism and suspicion, all of which can literally be toxic as the body pumps out potent fight-or-flight chemicals, leading to higher mortality. Gay singles, beware.

Intimacy on the other hand can be therapeutically blissful. But too often we look only to certain kinds of relationships for this kind of connection. "A romantic relationship is only one of countless ways of experiencing the healing power of love and intimacy," writes Ornish. What's most important, he maintains, is that *"we can only be intimate to the degree that we are willing to be open and vulnerable."*

As my own boundaries drop with Paul Barber, it becomes apparent that you *can* pay for that experience. Unfortunately, for many guys the barriers bounce right back up as soon as the session begins drawing to a close.

Most men want to get off the table as soon as they come, Barber tells me. And yet that's exactly when he thinks they should lie still. He does not believe the experience ends or climaxes with ejaculation. That's when he thinks it begins. "You've come, *now* you're ready. Now we can finally deal with what's bothering you. That's when men start to tell their truth. You cradle them, you nurture them. But where do we get this in society? You meet someone, you take them home, they take you home, you eventually go to bed, you have sex however it gets defined. Do you talk about what's bothering you? No. It's usually, I don't like guests overnight, or what would you like for breakfast tomorrow, or what do you do?"

And it's little wonder we don't open up.

"We're very good at wounding, so why would you open up to me if you've been wounded every time you did that?"

I find myself applying this question not only to love for hire but also to the potential for emotional closeness with fuck buddies, and yes, even one-night stands.

"So how do we bring this awareness to men?" I ask.

He smiles.

"One man at a time."

10. Boyfriends and Husbands Don't Protect against AIDS

You think sex is about fun and games and love. Wrong!
Sex is about disease. Here's a little picture of herpes.

—Miss Chokesondick, *South Park*

I LIKE HAVING SEX without condoms.

I also like not having HIV, not taking HIV medication, and not having AIDS.

In this final chapter I have to put that on the table because if anyone were to make an argument about the benefits of a boyfriend, I would no longer buy the need for intimacy as a valid one. That is available through friendships, tricks, fuck buddies, and yes, even some whores—if you're open to it and make the effort.

But I might buy the argument that being in an LTR means you can safely fuck without condoms, and that is not an argument to dismiss lightly. However, it does assume that both men in the couple are HIV-negative, or both are HIV-positive and willing to take the risk of infecting each other with a different strain of the virus.

So why is this worthy of a chapter all to itself? Because sex without condoms is a reality of life, and so is HIV.

My Maiden Voyage

I remember well the first time I had unprotected sex. It was with a guy I met on Seattle public transit who wound up back at my hotel room. Hotel sex is great. Someone else has to deal with the sheets.

I'd rarely been fucked, but he was very into getting up my ass. There's something about a guy begging to get in there that proves difficult to resist. Still, I insisted on using a condom. He got inside me, with latex, and man did it hurt. We tried several times, but I just couldn't loosen up enough to get into it. He kept asking me to let him take the condom off. I kept saying no. Once again we tried with latex, and this time I had to escape to the bathroom. Leaning on the countertop and staring at my naked self in the mirror I talked myself down and breathed through my rising tension and anxiety at my failure to take it up the ass.

A few minutes later I returned to the ring and tried taking his cock by sitting on it. All of a sudden in it went like the most natural thing in the world. I went real slow, at my own pace, and fuck it was hot. I'd pull off when I got soft and stuff my cock into his mouth to get hard again. Then my ass went back on his dick, then off, and mine into his mouth, back and forth, making me harder and harder, even when he was inside me.

This didn't hurt. This was *awesome*.

"I'm going to come," he groaned as I gyrated downward.

My breath stopped.

"You're wearing a condom, right?"

His eyes opened in alarm.

"No. I thought you knew."

I pulled off. He came on his belly. We made out and my cum joined his shortly thereafter.

In that encounter, barebacking was an accident. I can't say the same for the second time, as this guy in Montreal teased my cockhead inside his asshole. The nonspecific urethritis I contracted put the scare into me; for a while. But if taking it up the ass was easier without a condom, fucking a guy with one proved impossible. Like many guys, my cock just wouldn't stay hard. A study published in 2003 looking at men in Toronto engaging in unprotected sex stated that a third of them complained of decreased stimulation because of condom use, often leading to loss of erection.

In other words, for some of us unprotected sex isn't just about what feels good. Sex just wasn't possible without it. And I'm sorry, I just don't buy arguments suggesting one stick with oral and hand jobs. Once you've experienced a really great topping or bottoming session, blow jobs and hand jobs just aren't going to count as sex anymore, not in the same way.

So how was I to reconcile this discovery, coupled with my inability to stay hard or take it up the ass with condoms, with a desire to remain HIV-negative? And if I were HIV-positive, how would I reconcile my condom conundrum with a desire to have great sex without infecting anyone else? Would I simply turn to barebacking with other poz guys?

Poz Party

Dating becomes "a little more complicated" after testing positive, says André Martin, one of three organizers of Party Poz in Montreal, a social event for HIV-positive men and their friends to mix and mingle in a casual social setting. "We did some research on the Internet and what we found on the Internet was sex and bareback parties for HIV-positive men, but we found nothing like what we wanted to do."

He was inspired to start Party Poz in part from a social event years earlier, organized for seropositive men to mix and mingle. "I was at the door, taking tickets, and there was a man who was shaking as he gave his ticket." It was the first time since the man's diagnosis four years before that'd he'd gone out to where meeting someone might be possible.

In his slightly broken English, Martin explains to me the fears some HIV-positive men have when it comes to dating. "The moment to tell the person you are HIV positive is always difficult to say and to receive. Many don't even tell and many people don't go out anymore. And when we tell I would say maybe 90 percent get a slap in the face. This is not an easy topic. This is still linked with sex, linked with a bad life. It brings judgment, even in the gay community."

And yet because becoming HIV positive can cause many to reevaluate their lives, their desires, and their priorities, Martin says that for some that can increase the desire for a long-term relationship. He himself has been seeing an HIV-negative guy for more than two years.

"The people I know who are HIV-positive they would all like the relationship, maybe more than non-HIV. More of my positive friends desire a relationship than non-positive friends. It gives a different way of seeing life, changes the way we fit in, so maybe we need to share while we are alive instead of thinking later we'll share. And as we are not perfect anymore, as we discover we are not perfect, with HIV or any big sickness it makes anyone feel this imperfection, there's always a guilt associated with it because we became imperfect. Our image does not fit the dream of what we would be. My theory is that it makes the HIV-positive more inclined to become involved in a relationship, at least in my mini group."

But while HIV may cause some poz guys to want a relationship for emotional reasons, for negative guys it might cause them to want a boyfriend as a form of protection against HIV.

In my own scenario, Hollywood-based ideals led me to believe that I would one day meet a kind and understanding partner with whom I would slowly develop a deep bond that transcended the need for hot sex off the bat and we would ease into our passion, settling for oral and hand jobs in the short-term. After being together for three months (the period during which HIV antibodies might not be detectable by testing) we'd both get tested, and when our negative results came in we'd laugh at those stuck using latex and start screwing like rabbits happily ever after.

In my mind, a monogamous relationship with another HIV-negative guy really was the answer.

But the knight in shining armor, riding a white stallion on which to whisk me away from bars and HIV and snide rejections, must have found someone better along the way. For those who are HIV-positive this is of course an extremely insulting concept, because it positions them as having a disease from which to be rescued by a boyfriend. At the height of the AIDS crisis, some even had a name for this strategy.

Marriage of Convenience

During the initial outbreak of AIDS in the very early '80s, theories abounded as to the nature of this syndrome. Many of the initial patients had sexual partners in common, too many to be considered coincidence. Whatever the cause of AIDS, sex was quickly isolated as the most likely and perhaps primary means of transmission.

During this period the Centers for Disease Control in Atlanta reported that the median number of lifetime male sexual partners for homosexual male patients with AIDS was 1,160. With no smoking gun, one theory was that repeated exposure to a series of STDs could be leading to the breakdown of the immune system in afflicted individuals. This information, and lack thereof, provided the basis for early AIDS prevention efforts.

Bathhouse aficionado and co-owner of Toronto's Spa Excess, Peter Bochove has been in the industry for more than thirty years and was on the front lines when the deaths started mounting.

"I got to see it all. More of it than other people who may not have known as many people as I did. Most of the people from the Richmond Street bathhouse are dead. The people I came out with, gone. An artist friend went blind, then he died. I know a singer who went deaf, then he died. Horrors."

He himself was spared because he took seriously some radical advice from a doctor after reading about "a strange skin condition" in the *Advocate* back in the very early '80s when the term *AIDS* did not yet exist and some referred to it as GRID (gay related immune deficiency). His seventy-year-old straight physician had suggested he start wearing a condom during sex. At first Bochove just laughed.

"A condom? That's for people like you," he said. "That's to keep from having a baby. I'm not using a fucking condom."

"How many people do you know that you've had sex with in your community?" the doctor pressed.

"Well that's just about everybody," Bochove admitted.

"Yes, that's what I hear, too. If this *is* sexually transmitted, and it's lethal, why don't you just humor me and use a condom?"

Bochove had no idea how to put one on. One of the nurses from down the hall had to show him.

Out in the field, many had never even heard of GRID, but indulged Bochove's sheathed cock after he explained the deal. But his safe sex education varied radically from the official outreach.

A brochure put out by AIDS Project/LA in May of 1983 listed several preventative measures people could take. They ranged from "eat a nutritionally balanced diet" to "reduce your number of sexual partners. Sex with multiple partners definitely increases your risk of disease. . . . The possibility of AIDS being sexually transmitted is still open to debate and must be decided on an individual basis."

The Public Health Service recommended that sexual contact be avoided with those known or suspected to have the syndrome.

Even after the virus was discovered and an antibody test developed to detect it, some also theorized that it was *repeated* exposure to a significant amount of the virus that led to the onset of infection. In 1986, another AIDS-prevention brochure had in bold letters: "Limit Your Number of Partners!"

Many took that message seriously.

"Marriage of convenience" is what Douglas Sadownick called it in a piece he wrote for the October 29, 1985, issue of the *Advocate*. He describes himself as part of a "new batch of gay men . . . in their mid-20s and younger who see the health crisis, *not* Stonewall, as the decisive historical force shaping their identity" and refers to "health at all costs" as the "pressing motto" of his time.

"The sex was just lousy, but monogamous," he writes of the budding boyfriend relationship. "The arrangement was begun to keep our sex lives healthy, if not altogether sexy."

Fear of AIDS prompted them to start the relationship and to stick with it through rocky times. "The health crisis refereed as the built-in 'marriage counselor' of the '80s."

To breakup was seen to be courting death in the gay dating world, even though by the time the article was written the AIDS virus had been identified, a test was available to detect antibodies to the virus, and condom use was being touted as a means of protection. But the idea of relationship safety had taken hold.

There were ads like "Love won't keep you safe—but a rubber will," aimed at couples like Sadownick and his partner who might think that a relationship meant they were sheltered from a virus that could incubate for years and might already be in their system from previous liaisons. And there were definite attempts to counter the return of the stigma of gay sex as AIDS organizations put out brochures with messages like

"AIDS has been used to resurrect old guilts . . . but gay sex is a good and healthy thing and AIDS does not prove that it isn't." Some were promoting safe sex as hot sex, with "endorsements" like "I came in a condom—the very first time!"

God knows I didn't. And yet I grew up believing that it would be that easy, this message filtered into my brain through sex ed class and later advertisements, drumming condom use into my head as a must, that safe sex was hot sex, when it fact it wasn't necessarily so, not for a lot of guys.

Getting Fucked vs. Getting Fucked Over

According to the study *Renewing HIV Prevention for Gay and Bisexual Men,* which looked at both singles and couples, "one of the most consistent findings in HIV research is the tendency of couples, whether homosexual or heterosexual, to shift away from safe sex over time." Numerous other studies support this finding.

In some cases this is "negotiated safety," where partners determine their HIV status, and if it's the same, proceed with unprotected sex with each other. But the decision to drop condoms in a couple often does *not* follow negotiation but rather at times relies on nonverbalized assumptions. In some cases the mere *anticipation* that the relationship was getting serious led to dropping condoms, as did an *assumption* of monogamy. There are also cases of couples who know they have different HIV statuses, so one man takes on the top role as a form of protection (a risky strategy).

So why does this happen? Unlike for me, it's not just about being able to get and stay hard, or even extra physical stimulation. Dropping condoms has come to signify in some instances a certain level of trust. There were participants in the study who reported that refusing to drop condom use was taken as a sign of infidelity, otherwise there would be no need to keep using latex.

The result of all of this? "Several study participants seroconverted during the early stages of relationship development."

In these instances there was a *perception* of safety offered by a boyfriend. It's a notion dating back to the very beginning of the AIDS crisis, one that's left a huge impact on the state of gay coupling and which has dramatically increased the pressure for gays to get into relationships. This notion has also, arguably, become counterproductive in some instances in maintaining safe-sex practices both for singles and couples.

So basically if I want a satisfying sex life and I want to stay negative, I'm pretty fucked, single or otherwise. And if I were positive, and didn't want to infect anybody else while still getting to have a decent love life, I'd be equally fucked.

At least that's how I felt until relatively recently.

Until I started looking for intimacy in unlikely places.

The Wonder of an STR (Short-Term Relationship)
The last time I had unprotected penetration was with David. I met him at Toronto Pride 2003 and we had great, sweaty, sketchy sex after dirty dancing for hours at one of the

weekend's circuit parties. I just assumed he was going to be a one-night stand, and that he'd go back to British Columbia and quickly forget all about me. Then I ran into him again the following year, at the same event.

"Oh my god, you're the guy with the hilarious picture of you and a life-size cutout of Reese Witherspoon!" he shouted above the circuit beats, dragging me over to his friends. "This is the Hungarian guy I told you about!"

We wound up back at my place for a second time, toasting our first anniversary by soaking together in the tub and listening to *The Very Best of Sheryl Crowe*. And then we had sweaty, sketchy, unprotected sex for the second year in a row. I barbecued a veggie burger for him the next day, walked him back to his hotel, kissed him good-bye, and went to see *Shrek II* with a buddy.

But that was not that.

In "Single Gay Men," Andrew Hostetler found that his "respondents by no means felt alone in their singlehood. Forty-seven point nine percent stated that most of their gay friends are single. . . . But although the men seem to believe that they are in good company, the process of coming to terms with single status—and of explaining it to oneself—remains a largely solitary process."

This has been my experience, but I no longer feel like I can live this in isolation. The founders of the homophile organization the Mattachine Society in the '50s understood the importance of unity and camaraderie. In a room of lit candles, standing in a circle and holding hands, they pledged, "We are sworn that no boy or girl, approaching the maelstrom of deviation, need make that crossing alone, afraid and in the dark ever again. In these moments we dedicate ourselves once again to each other in the immense significance of such allegiance, with dignity and respect, proud and free."

In this spirit, half-a-century later, I apply this not to the transition of coming out of the closet but to my love life as a single gay man. A boyfriend does not guarantee protection from HIV, and even if it did, I don't have one to help me through my desire to have fun *and* stay HIV negative (and if I were positive, my desire to have fun and not pass HIV onto anybody else). But if my theory of intimacy and trust within casual encounters is true, at least in some instances, then that is where I will turn.

After David flew back to Vancouver I wrote him the following email:

Hey Stud,

Well that was a happy and unexpected one-year anniversary celebration. Merci beaucoup. I was very tempted to call you the next day after seeing Shrek II, *which was hilarious. Loved Jennifer Saunders as the fairy godmother. Anyway, I didn't call because I figured we'd probably end up back in the sack, and doing the nasty without condoms again, which I've promised myself over and over I wouldn't do anymore (a promise I seem to keep breaking). I know you get tested every three months, as do I, but one of these days our tests are going to come back positive unless we change our behavior. I'm not even sure if it's appropriate for me to be writing this to you as we don't really know each other, but all I know is that two years in a row you've brought me great moments of happiness during Pride, and I was so impressed that you remembered that I was Hungarian, not to mention Reese Witherspoon, and that you told your friends about me. That was really nice, and I was just left with the urge to follow up in some capacity. Thanks again for letting me fuck your hot ass. I loved hearing you moan and staring into your eyes while I squeezed my cock inside of you.*

S.

PS what's your last name?

At the most, I expected he might send me some sort of nasty response, telling me to mind my own business, or more likely that he'd get the email and promptly delete it, never to speak with me again. To my surprise, he not only wrote back, but we now chat on the phone every few weeks, and I'm finding the long distance is actually giving me a sense of safety in opening up in ways I might not otherwise. I find that honesty is slowly creeping into my interactions with local Toronto boiz as well. It's also the last time I've barebacked. Being open with him strengthened my resolve to not have unprotected sex. For a year I just didn't fuck. Temporarily taking this activity off the menu helped take the pressure off. And while Viagra helped little in my condom conundrum, a friend told me about having similar erectile problems and how he used large condoms to help. I've taken his advice, and found the upgrade helps keep the condom from pinching off my blood flow. Thank you friendship!

There have also been some one-night stands that have helped me ease into my condom comfort. There was the guy who loved being fingered but was leery of getting fucked, though he was willing to try. I never did penetrate him with my cock, but I did stay *really* hard with the large condom on as I teased his hole with my shaft. It was such a relief to not go limp inside latex. There was also the guy who said "we can go as slow as you want. There's no rush." He gave me not only this verbal affirmation but also the space and time to feel anxious and to let that anxiety mix with my rising sexual excitement. That was a fantastic night, and I think his words will be with me always as one of the nicest things a guy has ever said to me, and of way more meaning than when he said "I love you" as my fingers worked his hairless ass (although that meant something, too). And in terms of taking it up the butt myself, a big thank-you to yet another Toronto-based sacred intimate, Michael Baker, whose anal massages are the best prostate stimulation I've ever had.

I guess I've found some white knights along the way after all. Maybe I even *am* the white knight from time to time.

For a Night or for a Lifetime

I'm not saying opening up to a stranger will always go so smoothly, or always feel so positive, at least in the short term.

Nor am I entirely sure why it was so important for me to write to David, and not the other guys I screwed around with sans condoms, but I think it had to with my attempts to reach beyond the cavalier attitude we often have toward our casual sex partners. It was also a letter to *moi-même*, a reminder that I had to take better care of myself, and others.

This intertwines with something my friend Michael Rowe said to me that started a mind shift away from devaluing even the most passing of encounters.

"When you're with someone—whether for a night or for a lifetime—your responsibility is to honor the person you're holding in your arms, however briefly, and to make them feel glad they're there with you."

I'd *never* heard anyone talk like that before.

I take this message from him particularly seriously. In his own writing he has shared in intimate detail the complexities of navigating his relationship with his husband of twenty years, and how they've supported each other in ways that demonstrated a deep-seated respect and friendship. It's also clear that he lives a life full of broad definitions of love and what it means to be family. This is not only evidenced by the titles of two collections of his nonfiction writing, *Looking for Brothers* and *Other Men's Sons,* but also in the way he and his husband have taken on the role of mentor to several young men and in one case, become surrogate parents.

I doubt he even fully realizes how much his words have impacted me.

For a night or for a lifetime . . .

Until then only "happily ever after" seemed worthy of such noble treatment. Yet he was so earnest and sincere that I began to forget my philosophy of "you're responsible for your own orgasm."

Just as there is no such thing as "just" friends, there is no such thing as "just" sex. It is a wild and crazy thing to intertwine our bodies and penetrate as we do, to be inside someone and to let someone else in.

And there is more at stake than a few broken hearts and wounded egos. We need to start acknowledging the importance of our casual partners, whether we are fucking out of lust or love or need or loneliness. After all, why should we bother protecting ourselves or each other if indeed we and our partners for the night, for the hour, for the quickest of quickies are merely the means to shooting a load or another notch on the bedpost? If indeed a trick is less of a *person* than a boyfriend?

Long-term couples sometimes get infected by relying on love and trust and reacting to insecurity and possibly jealousy.

Short-term lovers should protect each other's hearts, bodies, and souls by showing caring and empathy.

We are not just sisters.

We are brothers.

Epilogue

Good luck in the games.

—Muriel Heslop (aka Toni Collette),
Muriel's Wedding

O NE NIGHT WHILE I was leaning on the lit up bar at
Woody's I was chatting with an emergency room nurse,
and I asked him to tell me a crazy hospital story. At first he
seemed hesitant, but I could tell from the look on his face that
he remembered a jewel, and with a little prodding, he shared
it with me.

A guy was rushed into the ER suffering from heart failure.

There are all sorts of reasons why a heart can stop. Too much potassium. Not enough magnesium. Quivering ventricles or not enough blood in the system.

The nurse leaned in toward me, but his mind seemed far away. His shyness and forced campiness had vanished. He might as well have been wearing scrubs.

"We're going to crack him open," the doctor on duty told him.

"No, we are not," the nurse replied.

"Yes, we are."

"No, we are *not*," he insisted.

The doctor proceeded to make an incision into the side of the patient's torso and used a spreader to force the ribs apart. Because the nurse's hand and wrist were smaller, it was he who squeezed his fingers through the opening and cupped the organ that's said to be our emotional center, massaging it gently between his fingers and palm, careful not to use his thumb. He kept his patient alive, kept the blood pumping through a body that could not do it for itself.

It took seven minutes to get that man up the elevator, into the operating room, and onto life support. It takes longer for some of us to take a shower, but who would dare call that sliver of time insignificant? For the rest of that nameless patient's existence those pivotal minutes will literally be the defining ones of every moment that follows.

There's a shimmer in the nurse's eyes as he concludes the tale.

"For seven minutes, I held a man's heart, in my hand."

As a single gay man I think of this story often, as well as the lesson it offers. By believing that love is a hierarchy to be climbed it devalues the love that *is* in my life, in the shape it *actually* takes, for the amount of time it *does* last. By believing in romance, and that it should lead to a long-term relationship in order to have value, I devalue these encounters further when they don't live beyond the initial flame.

And yet there have been one-night stands that have changed my life. And fuck buddies. And friends. Where do these sit on the relationship hierarchy? Below marriage. Below boyfriends. We say "just" friends and "just" sex. According to the hierarchy, these loves are either inconsequential or are simply part of growing up, until I mature into "real" love. And yet these men have played significant parts in my life, some in dramatic ways, others every so slightly. But it's amazing what an impact even a shift of a single degree can have. Draw a line along that new trajectory, and five years down the road you're in a completely different spot than you would otherwise have ended up in. You're also a very different person.

I pause to reminisce about a few of the men who have altered my heading.

There was the first guy I ever had sex with, which allowed me to finally get on with my love life. He's now married and has a kid. Then there's Kevin, the gay roommate who was the first person I ever came out to, the first friend I've ever had sex with, the first man I ever truly fell in love with instead of crushing on, and who, for whatever reason, fifteen years after we first met, still finds my advice, friendship, and company of use in his life.

When I was twenty-four there was, of course, the twenty-year-old *XY* magazine model who stole my heart in San Francisco and sent me on a romantic high through a combination of youthful charm and prominent cheekbones, not to mention my own shock at having successfully attracted a guy who looked like *that*.

At long last I knew it could be done.

There was also the fellow I met in Seattle, who liked to call himself the "Ghetto Cowboy," his rockin' go-go boy body and rhythmic moves sending me to Uranus and back. The variety of positions over six nonstop hours left every muscle in my body aching deeply and my psyche soaring in the newfound experience of what mind-bending sex was really like.

So *that's* what all the fuss is about!

I even sent that one a postcard.

I'll also never forget the three-day affair in Bangkok, with an Israeli tourist, who taught me to open my heart again after years of bruising had swelled it shut. I haven't spoken with him since. All the same, the photo of us hugging and grinning made it into a picture frame.

And then there was Reggie.

He was an adequate lay. A nice guy. Not my dream man, but the words "good enough" certainly applied. As I put my shoes back on at 4 AM on that fateful night/morning, and walked out his apartment door, for the first time in my life I neither offered my number nor did I have any desire to call him after he gave me his.

In the past I would've rung him up, just to see where that night's chemistry, be it physical or verbal, could go. The mere receipt of a phone number was encouragement enough. After all, a guy wouldn't scribble down his digits for me unless he wanted to see me again. It took me a while to learn this exchange of paper scraps (now replaced by punching numbers into one's cell phone, or perhaps swapping email addresses) was more often than not a polite formality that did not guarantee me anything, let alone a return phone call. As the rejections piled up as quickly as the slips of paper, so, too, did my hesitancy at each new encounter to expect something beyond the moment. But still there was this urge, this painful need, to at least try.

Until Reggie.

I left with a lightness in my chest.

I'm still not sure how, but I'd done it.

I'd transitioned.

We'd had a fun time, and I was delighted to leave it at that. I had no need to see or speak with him again, nor to somehow try to turn the experience into something more than what it was. I'd had one-night stands before, but this was the first time I was mentally and spiritually on board. All of a sudden the disappointment at the boys who'd failed to call me back vanished. I understood now. *This* is what they'd felt. It's not that I felt nothing or looked down on him or thought I could do better. But it was what it was, and it was enough.

In some strange way, I was freed.

We were temporary companions on a journey too often trod alone.

I'm not saying that this brief interlude of inner peace was not broken by long draughts of desperate thirsting for the much coveted boyfriend. But after a while I stopped pseudo-stalking attractive model/waiters by memorizing their work schedules and coincidentally dragging friends out for a meal during their shifts.

Instead, I pursued my own interests, put more time into family and friends, focused on my writing, slowly settling into the quiet calm and comfort of being a single gay man.

To reduce this process to a couple of paragraphs is to greatly simplify the trials and tortures that went along the way, such as having my heart bruised by the friend who was "perfect" for me, except for the fact that he had no interest in our naked bodies pressing against each other. And the previously mentioned hottie *XY* model from San Francisco kept me on an emotional tightrope when he'd grace me with a call once or twice a year. There was also my drunken breakdown as I sobbed and vomited in the parking lot outside my brother's wedding reception because I'd refused to invite anyone as a date except a boyfriend, and since I was single, there I was, surrounded by family, and feeling all alone, wishing my friend Vance was by my side.

My mother rubbed my back and called for an ambulance.

"He'll be fine," the paramedic assured her, ambulance siren

silent but lights still flashing behind him. "He just needs to sleep it off."

In a way he was right.

I look back on my past desperation like it was some kind of dream and am shocked when, on occasion, it still rears its head.

"I used to watch this one couple come to yoga class every Saturday morning," a friend was telling me as we walked through a park, relating a tale about these two hunky dudes. "They'd be all happy and couply, and it was nauseating." I was about to laugh until he gripped me by the arm and stopped us in mid-walk, staring me in the eye. "When's it going to be *my* turn to be nauseating?"

The moment was both funny and poignant, for I had to answer in all honesty, "I know exactly how you feel."

Those two hunks were the poster boys of the dream life, happy, attractive, successful, and in love. But that, of course, is what we see on the outside.

When they split, my friend confessed, "I felt bad. I felt like I broke them up. I *wished* them broken up, and then it happened."

Once again, I laugh at the poignancy of his words, and I try to remind myself that there is a lesson in such experiences. When I am jealous of someone else's relationship, or find myself turning into a teenage girl again over a guy that I'm crushing on and want to possess, I now know that something lies beyond these uncomfortable emotions. They are in part fuelled by a fantasy, and thankfully they will not last forever. I can say this because I've been through it now many times before. In other words, I'm not just using the narrative solution in hindsight anymore. I'm using past experience to project ahead.

I think of a line from Paul Monette's award-winning autobiography, which chronicles his struggles with his sexuality, his family, and having AIDS. In *Becoming a Man: Half a Life Story,* he writes, "It was only by seeing it as a quest that I got through so many lonely nights in the bars."

A quest of course implies some sort of final outcome, like finding the elusive Holy Grail, which for him was "two men in love and laughing." And he did indeed find his laughing man, and in so doing, comes to a narrative solution of his own for the painful years he spent in the closet.

"It all seems so inevitable in hindsight, meeting the one person who would make those twenty-five years of pain bearable at last. Because if the slightest thing had happened any differently in my checkered life, I wouldn't have been there to meet Roger that Sunday night on Revere Street. That much fate I believe in, the torturous journey that brings you to love, all the twists and near misses. Somehow it's all had a purpose, once you're finally real."

It is that last sentence that I find myself identifying with, for it encapsulates how I now feel about myself, having arrived in my singlehood. I'm finally real. It's a theme that crops up with longtime singles, and not just in the work of Andrew Hostetler.

From his work on straight singles in the '70s, researcher Peter J. Stein viewed "the never-married, who choose alternate paths of adult life not as deviants . . . but as conscious actors who occupy new roles in one or more areas of life." He references another study, "Career Strategies of the Never Married," which states: "As these singles approached 30, many . . . began to reevaluate their lives . . . [recognizing] the possibility that they might never marry and that they themselves had the responsibility for designing meaningful lives."

For myself this includes looking at how, instead of coming out of the closet to be myself, I have spent more than a decade constructing the facade of the person I thought gay guys would want to date.

I tried everything, from joining groups, to cutting my puffy hair, to lowering my standards, to not having sex right away, to having sex right away, to speed dating, to giving out my number, to getting the other guy's number, to focusing on personality, to not giving anyone a chance, to giving everyone a chance, to demanding physical perfection, to being open to chest hair, to waiting to have sex, to not waiting to have sex, to snorting coke (only twice), dropping E, dancing shirtless, getting a tan, Nair-ing my ass, fucking without condoms, moving into a condo, buying new furniture, putting product in my hair, and even reading frigging *Harry Potter*.

And the truth is, while they may be de rigueur, I just don't like *Harry Potter* books.

They're poorly written.

As for the drugs, sex, and body fascism, I have found both healing and wounding within this milieu. At times I've bared myself and been scorched in hostile terrain. Fearing exposure, I've dived back into my shell, suffocating under new layers of reinforced armor. But there have also been really wonderful moments, and guys, along the way. Even the harshest of deserts are teeming with life that's evolved not only to survive in such a seemingly stark habitat but to thrive.

Unfortunately the oasis many of us crave is elusive, and dating can too often feel like an emotionally deadly game of predator and prey. But if we were a little more symbiotic, instead of treating each other like undesirable parasites, we'd be doing each other and ourselves a huge favor.

In my own journey, I've had many boys who have changed my life for the better, and not necessarily because of a fun experience. The hard times probably taught me more than the romantic ones. And to further grow, I have sought professional help, both traditional and unorthodox.

Therapy has forced me to acknowledge a mélange of fears and anxieties that arise when I have sex. Can I trust this guy to wear a condom? Can I trust myself to kick him out if he asks to take it off? Can I relax enough to be penetrated? Can I get out of my head and connect with my body, and his, staying hard enough to penetrate him with a condom on?

These are not the thoughts of the pornlike sex god I wanted to be. This realization brought on bouts of physical nausea. I am not who I thought I was. Mentally this admission is like walking through the valley of darkness. But day by day I am growing more comfortable with my discomfort. The valley of darkness gives way to the valley of shadow. The valley of semi-shade is just ahead. I begin to fantasize what it might be like to tell a guy that I'm feeling anxious, that stroking my back and staring into my eyes helps warm up my body and gets me out of my head, that I'm a skittish cat that can be fiercely affectionate and sexual when coaxed into trusting, even if it's for one night alone.

So goes the quest for the authentic self, the person that we want our lover to love, but which we often hide from others for fear that we are at heart unlovable. To find and calibrate this inner compass requires stripping back the layers of the facade we construct starting in childhood as we learn what behaviors earn us rewards, and which shower us in guilt, shame, and scorn. I thought a boyfriend would one day dig through the muck to pull forth the diamond beneath.

Fortunately I can do much of the digging on my own, and when I need help, there are companions in this life, both long- and short-term, from family to friends to therapists to fuck friends to sex workers to one-night stands.

To minimize their importance in concordance with a hierarchy is to adhere to a fictitious one-size-fits-all roadmap to intimacy and contentment. We don't expect the same workout routine or diet to work for everybody in the same way, why would we think a single roadmap could pave the way for emotional fulfillment for every person on the planet? That was tried, remember?

It's called heterosexuality.

Acknowledgments

THERE ARE MANY PEOPLE to thank. For their time and honesty, all the men who I interviewed for this book. For their support and advice, my family (see dedication) and friends: Michele Collins, Craig Dale, Nicole Demerse, Neil Fleming, Howard Kane, Nick Kazamia, Jill Kinsella, Lance Lamore, Sean Ling, Cheryl Misener, Andrew Nichols, Michael Rowe, Robin Rowland, and Matt Siefert. For giving me this opportunity, along with the right mix of free rein and amazing guidance, my publisher, Matthew Lore. For a fabulous copy edit, David Coen. For preserving so much of gay history, the Canadian Lesbian and Gay Archives. For good times and bad, all the guys I've ever gone on a date and/or had sex with. Most of all I want to thank my friend and mentor Mitchel Raphael for assigning me the story "What If You Are Gay and Single Forever?" for *fab* magazine's 2004 Valentine's issue. This book grew out of that. May the force be with you.

Made in the USA
Lexington, KY
24 November 2012